Overcome Procrastination God's Way!

Why Put Off For Tomorrow What God Can Do Today?

From an Overcoming Procrastinator
CLARENCE J. PARKS, J.D., M.Div.

Bowie, Maryland

Unless otherwise noted, all Scripture quotations are from the
King James Version of The Bible.

Overcome Procrastination God's Way!
ISBN Number 978-0-9832-3370-1

Published by i611 Press, LLC
Bowie, Maryland 20721
www.i611press.com

Cover and Interior Layout Design by Gloria Marconi
Author Photograph by Ron Thomas

Hand-Drawn Illustrations by Otis Blackmon
Computer Illustrations by istockphoto.com

Printed in The United States of America
by Signature Book Printing, Inc.
www.sbpbooks.com

†

Dedication

I dedicate this book to my Aunt Elizabeth Todd,
and my Aunt Fannie Singletary,
sisters who passed away in 2010.

I shall never forget you.

†

Acknowledgements

To my mother, Barbara D. Parks-Lee, who continuously encouraged me to "keep writing." Thanks, Mom, for your mother's love.

To my father, St. Clair Parks, Jr., a man of great wisdom, thanks for being such an inspiration to me. And my sister, Claire, thanks for being the wonderful, caring individual you are.

To my Granny-Poo, you know how special you are to me. I love you very, very much and give honor to you.

To my step-father, Willie Lee, thanks for encouraging me by asking, "How's your book coming?" I appreciated that.

To my father in the ministry, Pastor John R. Brown, Sr., thanks for being such a great motivator especially early on when I didn't fully believe in myself. I just want to thank you being such a great example.

To Apostle Jesse and Pastor Sophonia Stevens, of Shekinah New Life Ministries of The Lord Jesus Christ, thanks for being such great spiritual leaders. You are both heaven-sent.

Special thanks to all my family members, The Peace and Power Ministries church family, my friends and Brother's of Kappa Alpha Psi Fraternity, Inc. who have given moral and spiritual support during the course of my journey.

Also, to all of the my former English Teachers from DCPS' H.D. Woodson Senior High School, Ms. Helen Cleveland, Mr. Rufus Horton, Mother Emma Brown, and Dr. Francis J. Carter, thanks for imparting in me a desire to write and thanks for dedicating your lives to educating young minds. God has special blessings stored up for you.

And especially to my dear wife Chellie for encouraging me throughout this entire process and listening tirelessly when I needed to talk through what God was giving me. Thank you sweetie for being you and putting up with me. I love you immensely.

†

Table of Contents

FOREWORD

PREFACE

INTRODUCTION: No Lack: The Basic Standard of Life

PART I
The Underlying Spiritual Root Causes of Procrastination

CHAPTER 1: What's Taking So Long? | 1
Procrastination Defined | 5

CHAPTER 2: Vision | 8
Envision No Lack | 12

CHAPTER 3: Decisions, Decisions, Decisions | 17
Decisions Defined | 18
Knowledge of God's Will | 20
Wisdom | 22
Spiritual Understanding | 26

CHAPTER 4: Fear, Worry and Shame | 29
Fear | 29
Worry | 31
Shame | 34

CHAPTER 5: Confrontation | 39
The Big Show Down | 41
Confront Fear and Worry | 43
Confront Shame | 48
Practical Steps to Confront | 53

†

Table of Contents

PART II | 57

A Practical Guide to Dig Out From the Past, Manage the Present, and Enter Into the Future

CHAPTER 6: Order | 59

Understand Order | 60

Dig Out From The Past | 62

Manage The Present | 63

Enter The Future | 66

CHAPTER 7: The 777 Plan™ | 71

7 Areas of Desire | 74

7 Actions | 78

7 Months to Achieve | 102

CHAPTER 8: Desire and Diligence | 107

Consider The Ant | 109

Be Realistic | 113

Fight One Battle at a Time | 114

Be Thorough | 117

Beware of Bad Desires | 120

CHAPTER 9: Vitality and Virtue | 129

Get Empowered | 133

Take a Sabbath | 135

Take Action | 138

EPILOGUE: The Process of Change | 141

†

Foreword

Greetings! I am Willie Jolley and I want to let you know that when you read Clarence Parks' book, *Overcome Procrastination God's Way!* your life is going to change.

Believe me when I tell you, I know something about change because I wrote about it in my book *It Only Takes a Minute to Change Your Life.* By reading this book you will learn how to get moving in the direction you want to go in.

Many moons ago, I met Clarence when he was about ten years old. My mom, the late Catherine B. Jolley, and his dad, St. Clair Parks, Jr., were fellow World Bookers. Since then, I have watched a vibrant young man mature into a powerful preacher, a thoughtful teacher, and an awesome author. For these reasons, I am excited to write the foreword of Clarence's new book, *Overcome Procrastination God's Way!*

In his book, Clarence provides helpful strategies on how to break the back of slack so that you can enter into the land of no lack. That's where we should all strive to arrive.

After reading his book, you will learn how to get there because Clarence provides you with both a spiritual and practical guide on how to overcome procrastination. I have not seen that in any other book on the subject. If you do what Clarence prescribes, you will be motivated, and will have all the tools you need to finally get past the past, manage your affairs well in the present, and start making your move into the future.

The timing for Clarence's book is impeccable because there are so many people who are seeking new ways to overcome procrastination. If you are one of those people then you are well on your way to achieving your goals.

Way to Go Clarence! Thanks for sharing your gift to the world! *Overcome Procrastination God's Way!* is going to help a lot of people.

Willie Jolley

World Renowned Motivational Speaker and Best-Selling Author of *A Setback Is A Setup for a Come Back*, *It Only Takes a Minute to Change Your Life* and *An Attitude of Excellence*

Preface

Procrastination is the number one killer even more than cancer and AIDS put together. It causes the premature death of thoughts, dreams and desires that were intended to become realities. It is the cause of so much drudgery and unhappiness in our lives, especially when it lingers on and on. It drains us of the power to live peacefully in the present and progressively in the future. Instead, with procrastination, we end up living painfully yet presently in the past.

This struggle has plagued us for far too long. As a result, we need a strategy to help us to triumph over this seemingly never ending cycle of inaction.

Throughout history, many studies have been conducted and many books have been written to identify the root causes and provide strategies to overcome procrastination. However, very few attempts have been made to address the underlying root causes of procrastination from a spiritual perspective.

That is why I wrote this book. I am an overcoming procrastinator and in my quest to overcome, I could not find any material which dealt with my problem spiritually.

The spiritual basis of the book is found in Joshua 18:1-10 which provides insight into why seven of the twelve tribes of Israel procrastinated on taking possession of the Promised Land.

With that spiritual backdrop, we will analyze what Joshua meant when he asked, "Why are you slack to go and possess the land, which the Lord God of your fathers has given you?"

Since that question is still relevant for us today, this book will attempt to dig deeper into why "we" are slack to take possession of what is rightfully ours in life. It will expose the underlying spiritual root causes of procrastination and it will provide strategies to overcome those things. In addition, this book will adopt the 777 strategy that Joshua provided to the seven procrastinating tribes.

Specifically, Part I of this book identifies the spiritual root causes of procrastination while Part II provides a strategy to dig out from the past and manage the present so that we can enter into the future.

†

Why Put Off For Tomorrow What God Can Do Today?

Jesus said, "No procrastination.
No backward looks.
You can't put God's Kingdom
off till tomorrow.
Seize the day."

Luke 9:62 (*The Message Bible*)

†

Introduction

No Lack— The Basic Standard of Life

For the Lord thy God bringeth thee into a good land…
thou shalt not lack anything in it.

Deuteronomy 8:7-9

There they were. After forty years of wandering in the wilderness, they found themselves standing at the threshold of taking possession of the Promised Land. As they stood there, Moses reminded them that it was God Who brought them to the good land that lacked nothing. However, first, they had to cross the River Jordan, topple the walls of Jericho as well as conquer some unforeseen enemies before they could take possession of what was rightfully theirs. In order to take those final steps, they needed to have vision; make God Decisions; confront hindrances; gain and maintain order; have desire and diligence; and possess virtue and vitality.

Taking the necessary and final steps was well worth the effort because God did not make a promise that He did not intend to keep. God went every step of the way with them. Therefore, there was no time for *procrastination* because the land of *no lack* was ready and waiting for them.

God's will for humankind has not changed. God still intends for us to lack nothing in every area of our lives and is still willing to go every step of the way with us. God's supply of available resources is still sufficient to fulfill every one of our desires and He has provided us with a strategy to overcome procrastination so that we can live the no lack lives that He has promised. God's strategy requires that we:

- **Have Vision**
- **Make God Decisions**
- **Confront Hindrances**
- **Gain and Maintain Order**
- **Have Desire and Diligence**
- **Have Virtue and Vitality**

By implementing God's strategy, we will break the back of slack and overcome procrastination. However, we will have to cross our own Jordan Rivers, fight our own battles of Jericho as well as conquer other hostile enemies which loom underneath and cause us to pause in going forward in our lives.

When we do these things we will be able to:

- **Dig Out from the Past**
- **Manage the Present Effectively**
- **Enter into a Future that Lacks Nothing**

God will be with us every step of the way as we commence our journey. However, we should keep in mind that this journey is a marathon and not a sprint. Nonetheless, if we endure, we will begin to live progressively and peacefully in the future instead of presently and painfully in the past. The latter is filled with unfulfilled obligations, unnecessary expense, disappointment and dreams which constantly are deferred because of our chronic procrastination. However, our lives will be filled with joy, peace, and love and *all* of our desires–in *every* area of life–will be fulfilled if we choose to overcome procrastination God's way.

Since no lack is God's basic standard, we will prosper in every area of our lives. However, it is important to note that financial prosperity is not enough because there are many who have prospered financially but still lack in other areas of life.

Let me ask you ...

Food For Thought

- **Is every area of your life complete, balanced and fulfilled?**
- **If not, why not?**
- **If not, what's taking you so long?**
- **What's causing you to procrastinate on living a balanced life that lacks nothing?**

†

Part I

The Underlying Spiritual Root Causes of Procrastination

We procrastinate mainly because of what we have going on inside of us. Simply put, we are slack, sluggish or slothful because we either have a negative self perception; we are indecisive; or we are afraid, worried or ashamed.

In fact, those factors are some of the underlying spiritual root causes of procrastination and must be dealt with spiritually. This section of the book will attempt to do just that.

We will investigate how to deal with the things that loom and roar underneath and cause us to pause on going forward toward what God has arranged and ordained for our lives. At the same time, we will consider scripturally-based strategies which will help us to confront and overcome those things. Ultimately, we will break the back of slack and we will enter into the land of no lack.

†

Chapter One
What's Taking So Long?

And Joshua said unto the Children of Israel,
How long are you going to be slack to go to possess the land,
which The Lord God of your fathers hath given you?

Joshua 18:3

When Moses finished his remarks on the wilderness side of the River Jordan, his journey ended. Then Joshua, the new leader of the Israelites, took over and was charged with taking them the rest of the way into the land that lacked nothing. Joshua led them across the River Jordan, conquered Jericho, and won all of the other battles that they were forced to fight. The only thing left for them to do was to take possession of what was rightfully theirs. Some of the tribes took possession right away, but the majority stayed right where they were. Seven of the twelve tribes did not take the final necessary steps and therefore did not take possession of the land that lacked nothing. Instead, they procrastinated and rested in the comfort zone at Shiloh (which means place of comfort).

Perhaps the seven procrastinating tribes opted for Shiloh because it was better than the wilderness that they had come out of. Or, maybe they were fearful and worried about what the future would bring. It is not completely clear why the seven tribes procrastinated, just as it is not completely clear why we do the same. However, Shiloh was not what God intended for them and is not what God intends for us. God intends for us to live no lack lives. So just as Joshua needed to understand why the seven procrastinating tribes were slack to go and possess the land, let me ask you the same question: *What's taking you so long? Why are you slack to go and possess the land—the no lack life that rightfully belongs to you?*

To be slack means we are feeble, weakened, idle, or faint. We usually become slack because we are displeased, fearful or unhappy about something. Those things loom underneath in our hearts, minds and souls and boil inside of us like something boiling in a pressure cooker. As a result, we procrastinate. We avoid work, physical exertion, or anything else that we perceive is painful or uncomfortable.

Some people equate slackness, slothfulness and sluggishness with laziness. However, we are not necessarily lazy. Rather, when those underlying spiritual root causes loom and roar underneath we become stifled from taking action. For example, in the case of the sloth and the slug, it is not laziness but fear, anxiety and sorrow looming underneath which causes us to pause from taking action. At the same time, we really do want to take action, but when we don't, we become more and more ashamed of ourselves. Again, it is not that we are lazy. Instead, we are just stifled by all we have going on deep down inside.

As a result, we experience further delay in taking action because we combine shame with fear and anxiety. That is not a good combination. Ultimately, our dreams get deferred and our desires get derailed because of those things that loom underneath. Proverb 21:25 says, *"The desire of the slothful killeth him; for his hands refuse to labour."* Also, Proverb 13:4 says, *"The soul of the sluggard desireth and hath nothing."*

It is frustrating to have a desire to take action but because we are so preoccupied with fear, worry or shame, we cannot move. Our desire to take action gets short-circuited and we never reach our intended goals. After a while, we become discouraged and we all but give up on our quest to live no-lack lives.

In addition, those underlying spiritual stumbling blocks also cause us to squander our most valuable resources: time, energy, money and opportunity. Proverb 18:9 says, *"He also that is slothful in his work is brother to him that is a great waster."* Ultimately, our lives spiral downward and become like a hedge of thorns. Solomon cautions us this way when he said:

I went by the field of the slothful, and by the vineyard of the man void of understanding: and lo, it was all grown over with thorns, and nettles had covered the face thereof was broken down. Then I saw, and considered it well: I looked upon it, and received instruction.

Proverbs 24:30-32

The mad cycle continues. Something looms underneath and causes us to pause. Then, stuff stacks up and backs up and we are barely able to manage our current obligations. Meanwhile, we are forced to put off the things that we want or need to accomplish in the present and in the future. Each round goes lower and lower and we acquiesce, we give up, or we give in, and ultimately the quality of our lives diminishes. At some point in this vicious cycle, we become impoverished in some way or another, and we continue to live below God's no lack standard of life. That is not what God intends for our lives.

Maybe that's what Joshua was so concerned about. Maybe he knew that if the seven procrastinating tribes continued to be slack, slothful, or sluggish, they would end up living below God's no lack standard and the quality of their lives would be diminished in some way or another. Perhaps, that's why he asked: *"How long are you going to be slack to go and take possession?"* Maybe the question was rhetorical, and was intended to get them to think about what was causing them to pause. Or, maybe it was intended to prod them into taking action. Either way, Joshua attempted to help the seven procrastinating tribes to break the back of slack so they could enter into the land of no lack. The land of no lack had already been conquered for them and the only thing left for them to do was to just take the first step.

Procrastination Defined

Now, before we go any further, let's explore what procrastination really is. Procrastination comes from two Latin root words: *pro* (to, toward or forward) and *cras* (tomorrow). The two meanings "toward tomorrow" put together means we put things off until tomorrow. Webster's dictionary defines procrastination as *putting something off until a later time; to delay*. In addition, we can use the terms procrastination, slack, slothfulness or sluggishness interchangeably because with each the end result is the same—we put something off until a later time. However, we should know that we do not put things off until tomorrow just because. Instead, we procrastinate because of the spiritual root causes which loom underneath in our hearts, minds or souls or because something else is out of order or unbalanced.

The seven procrastinating tribes *put off* taking possession of what God had promised them, and we put off living lives that lack nothing. Therefore, we should ask ourselves, "what is taking me so long?" Once we do that, then we should be willing to do something about it once and for all. We need to take action so that we can start living the lives that God has ordained for us. However, before we consider the solutions, let us address other possible reasons why we procrastinate. The seven procrastinating tribes may have put off taking possession of the Promised Land because they may have had a lack of vision; may not have made God decisions; may not have been able to confront difficult things; may not have had desire and diligence to finish what they started; or they may have run out of virtue and vitality. Again, it is not totally clear.

Therefore, it is worth exploring each one of these possibilities because most likely whatever caused them to procrastinate is what causes us to procrastinate.

Food For Thought

- **What's taking you so long?**
- **How long are you going to be slack, slothful or sluggish to live a life that lacks nothing?**
- **What's really causing you to procrastinate?**

- **What is looming underneath?**
- **Is it fear, worry or shame?**
- **Or is it something else?**

Prayer:

Father, I acknowledge that I have been slack, slothful or sluggish in taking possession of the life that lacks nothing that You have promised in Your Word.
Father, please help me to identify what causes me to procrastinate so that I can overcome them with your help.
Lord, You are my Rock and my Redeemer.
In Jesus' Name, I pray, Amen!

Summary of Scriptures:

Deuteronomy 8:7-9

Joshua 18:3

Proverb 21:25

Proverb 13:4

Proverb 18:9

Proverbs 24:30-32

Notes

†

Chapter Two
Vision

For the Lord thy God bringeth thee into a good land…
thou shalt not lack anything in it.

Deuteronomy 8:7-9

The seven procrastinating tribes may have been slack to possess the land because they may not have been able to envision themselves being in a better position than the one they were already in. Even though God had already communicated His vision of no lack through Moses, it is possible that they still could not fully see it for themselves. Therefore, they stayed right where they were. They stayed in the uncomfortable comfort zone at Shiloh. So it is with many procrastinators—we procrastinate because we cannot see a better way of doing things. This is especially the case when we experience difficult circumstances or if we have been procrastinators throughout the course of our lives. As a result, we end up lacking in some area of our lives.

To have vision means that we are able to see the mental image of a desired result. It is where we gain insight into where we are going and how we are going to get there. This vision is usually communicated through a word, thought or dream. However, the visions which yield the most positive results are those that are informed by reliable information. The source that informed the vision for the Israelites was The Word of God. In Deuteronomy 8:7-9, Moses reminded them that it was God who had spoken The Word; that it was His intent for them to live in the land of no lack. The heavenly vision, if believed and pursued, yields positive results—no lack in every area of life. God's vision for humankind has not changed. His Word is still the same, and He still desires that we should live lives that lack nothing.

What's Clouding The Vision?

And they brought up an evil report of the land
which they had searched unto the Children of Israel…
and we were in our own sight as grasshoppers,
and so we were in their sight.

Numbers 13:32-33

We procrastinate because we cannot fully grasp or fathom God's vision for our lives. For the Children of Israel, they were given a reliable vision based on reliable information—God's Word. However, they still put off taking a step towards making God's vision their reality. This may have been the case because their vision was clouded by a negative self-image handed down from the previous generation who saw themselves as grasshoppers instead of conquerors.

We are told in Numbers 13:32-33, that some spies were sent to spy out the land. When they got back from their mission, they gave an evil report—they saw some giants living in the land. When the spies saw them, they focused on the size of the giants and perceived themselves as being inadequate. Then they spread that negative perspective throughout the community by proclaiming that they were *"in their own sight as grasshoppers."* Their vision was clouded by the negative image they had of themselves and the gigantic challenges they faced. As a result, the Israelites began to believe that they would not be able to possess the land of no lack that God had promised them and because of that negative perspective—they didn't. In essence, they internalized the evil report and as a result that became their reality instead of God's vision.

So it is with us, when we see ourselves as grasshoppers, our negative self image ultimately becomes ingrained in our psyche. As a result, we begin to see ourselves and our abilities as being smaller than the vision that God sees for our lives.

In essence, we put off thinking bigger or reaching higher because we cannot fathom achieving anything beyond what we think about ourselves. At the same time we begin to believe that we cannot overcome the things that loom underneath or the gigantic challenges we face. We also begin to believe the enemy's unreliable messages when he whispers: "You know you'll never get beyond where you are right now" or, "It's too big or too hard" or, "You know you are not worthy, equipped or able to accomplish a life of no lack."

If we listen and choose to see ourselves that way, then, most likely, we will achieve what we see—little or nothing. However, all of this is hogwash because it is based on evil reports and unreliable information. There is nothing farther from the truth. We can get beyond where we are right now especially when we decide to see things the way God sees them. We are not grasshoppers; we are conquerors. In fact, according to Romans 8:37, we *"are more than conquerors."* Thus, we can un-cloud our vision by changing what we think and the way we think about ourselves. We can do this by focusing on God's heavenly vision of no lack which clearly has been articulated in the reliable and infallible Word of God.

However, if the choice to un-cloud God's vision is difficult to make, then there are a couple of things we can do to get going. For the seven procrastinating tribes who could not un-cloud God's vision for their lives, Joshua provided them with at least two suggestions. He suggested that they should:

- **Envision What a No Lack Life Looks Like**
- **Write It Down**

We should consider his suggestions.

Envision it! No Lack, Want or Void!

Go and walk through the land.

Joshua 18:8

As the seven procrastinating tribes sat idly at Shiloh, Joshua knew that it was time to take action. He suggested that they pick twenty-one men (three from each tribe) to go and walk through the land. In essence, he was suggesting that they should go and scope out the land that was before them, and then come back and describe what they saw. We should do likewise. We should go and take a mental walk and envision what a no lack life looks like for our lives. Can you envision your life lacking nothing in every area?

What would it look like if you were able to dig out from past due, unfulfilled desires and obligations; efficiently manage the present, while achieving your dreams and desires for the future? Can you see that for yourself in every area of your life? What do you think it will take for you to get there? If you can't fathom that, then you should ask yourself, why not? And then consider the possibility any way because all things are possible with God.

Write it Down

Write the vision, and make it plain upon the tables, that he may run that readeth it.

Habakkuk 2:2

Once we've envisioned our lives lacking nothing, then it is important to record what we saw. Why? Because thinking and dreaming is what procrastinators do best. We think and think and think and then think some more about what could, should or would be done. However, when we think so much, our previous thoughts get morphed together with our current thoughts because we have too many thoughts running through our minds. As a result, our thoughts do not become realities instead they vanish away.

However, the likelihood that our thoughts and desires will turn into realities increases when we write them down. This happens because the thoughts that once used to swirl around in the already crowded small space of our minds, get emptied out and begin to crystallize into possibilities.

Do You See What God Sees?

For I know the thoughts that I think toward you, saith the Lord, thoughts of peace, and not of evil, to give you an expected end.

Jeremiah 29:11

Let me ask you…

Food For Thought

- **Do you see what God sees for your life—no lack and peace?**
- **Or do you see your self lacking in some way?**
- **Are you a grasshopper or a conqueror?**
- **Do you believe that your life will get any better than it is right now?**

If you can see what God's sees, then you are well on your way to obtaining the no lack life that God has envisioned for your life. Even if you cannot see these things right now, that does not mean that you cannot change your perspective. I want to encourage you because whether you can see it or believe it or not, YOU CAN DO IT!

No lack is the expected end that God sees for you. Maybe you just need a little bit more information so that you can decide to do what needs to be done to un-cloud your vision, break the back of slack and begin to enter into the land of no lack. If that is what you want or need, then keep reading.

Prayer:

Father, I believe that the vision that You have for my life is much greater than the vision that I can see for myself. However, Lord, I need Your help to come against whatever is clouding my vision from seeing things the way You do. Father, I proclaim that I am not a grasshopper but instead I am more than a conqueror according to Your Word and I give You permission to fulfill the vision that You have ordained for my life. In Jesus' Name, I pray, Amen!

Summary of Scriptures:

Deuteronomy 8:7-9

Numbers 13:32-33

Romans 8:37

Joshua 18:8

Habakkuk 2:2

Jeremiah 29:11

†

Chapter Three
Decisions, Decisions, Decisions

Multitudes, multitudes in the valley of decision:
for the day of the Lord is near in the valley of decision.

Joel 3:14

One of the best steps we can take to overcome procrastination God's way is to decide to do so. For the seven procrastinating tribes, they could have entered into the land of no lack a lot sooner if they would have decided to get up and get going a lot sooner. The land had already been conquered and made available to them but for some reason, they either could not, or would not decide to go forward toward what God had ordained for them. Instead, they decided by default to stay at Shiloh, which was only intended to be a temporary resting place.

We do the same thing. Many of us decide by default to stay right where we are instead of deciding to take action to overcome procrastination, break the back of slack, and enter into the land of no lack. William James, who is often referred to as the father of modern psychology, once said, "When you have to make a choice and don't make it, that in itself is a choice." In other words, indecision is a decision, by default, to stay right where we are. As a result of indecision, we procrastinate and don't take action. I don't believe this is a conscious decision. Instead, I believe our psyche and desire are negatively affected by those things that loom and roar underneath. Therefore, we need to understand:

- **What a decision is**
- **Which decisions are the best decisions**
- **What helps us to make the best decisions**
- **What hinders us from making the best decisions**

Decisions Defined

Webster's Dictionary defines a decision as *a judgment or conclusion reached.* It is also defined as *a determination or firmness of mind.* It is where we are persuaded to take action by discerning what is best or right for us. Making a decision forces us to determine whether the information we have received is credible or true. Hence, we either decide for or against the information or we decide to not decide. If we decide to not decide then we actually decide by default to do nothing. President Theodore Roosevelt said, "In a moment of decision, the best thing you can do is the right thing to do. The worst thing you can do is nothing." Thus, if we want to overcome procrastination, we will need to discover what the "right things" are so we can decide to do them.

The Best Decisions are "God" Decisions

Information and ideas inform every decision. Bad or faulty information leads to bad or faulty decisions, but good information leads to "good decisions." However, good decisions are good but are not necessarily great decisions. Great decisions are God Decisions, and God Decisions are informed by God's Ideas. God's Ideas are God's thoughts, and His thoughts are found in God's Word—The Bible. When we are fully persuaded that God's Word brings us great results, then our decisions will be great. Therefore, God Decisions are the best decisions because when we make them, we will be able to overcome procrastination God's way; we will be able to dig out from the past, manage the present and enter into a future that lacks nothing; and we will be able to achieve great results!

What Goes Into Making "God" Decisions?

There are at least three things found in God's Word that will help us to make God Decisions:

- **Knowledge of God's Will**
- **God's Wisdom**
- **Spiritual Understanding**

Knowledge of God's Will

Then shall we know, if we follow on to know the Lord...

Hosea 6:3

To have knowledge of God's Will literally means we are fully acquainted with and we fully recognize what God's Will is for our lives. It goes beyond mere information. Instead, it is deeply embedded in our innermost being and provides us with an understanding of who God is and what He has specifically purposed for our lives from the inside out. With this knowledge, God connects and communicates with us and makes an imprint of "The Master's Plan" onto our souls. In fact, according to Proverb 2:10, possession of this kind of knowledge *"is pleasant to the soul"* because it brings such pleasant results. Proverb 24:14 says *"When thou hast found it, then there shall be a reward, and thy expectation shall not be cut off."* Therefore, with this knowledge, we will make the best decisions and we will get the best results. Finally, we will be able to overcome procrastination that is caused by indecision.

However, without knowledge of God's Will in our souls, we will not make the best decisions nor will we get the best results. Proverb 19:2 says, *"It is not good."* We will continue to be hindered by the bad or "just good" decisions we make. Or worse, we will not make any decisions at all, and that is never good because it can only lead to further procrastination. Ecclesiastes 11:4 (NIV) says, *"Whoever watches the wind will not plant; whoever looks at the clouds will not reap."* In essence, we will end up suffering from paralysis of the analysis because we will not "know" what God's Will is for our lives, or we will decide badly because we will not have the right information which leads to right results.

Knowledge of God's Will is obtained through the establishment and diligent maintenance of a close relationship with God through The Lord Jesus Christ. Jesus said:

> *All things have been entrusted and delivered to Me by My Father; and no one fully knows and accurately understands the Son except the Father, and no one fully knows and accurately understands the Father except the Son and anyone to whom the Son deliberately wills to make Him known.*
>
> Matthew 11:27 (AMP)

If we truly desire to have knowledge of (be fully acquainted with) God's will, then Christ will deliberately make The Father's will known to us. He does this from the inside out. He gives us a gnosis (*kno-sis:*

a knowing that God is there) in our souls. With this gnosis, He helps us to make God decisions. He helps us to navigate our way through the things that have caused us to procrastinate throughout the course of our lives. And, He helps us to find our way to the land of no lack. Is obtaining this knowledge easy? The answer is yes and no.

The answer is "yes" because at the moment we establish a relationship with God through Jesus Christ, He takes up residence in our souls by way of the Holy Spirit and we get knowledge (a gnosis; a knowing). But, the answer is also "no" because becoming aware of this knowledge takes a little bit more. It takes a revelation in our hearts and realization in our minds of the presence of God. With those things, we receive spiritual insight as to what decisions we should make and what steps we should take to dig out from the past, manage the present, and enter into a no lack future. Revelation comes through Godly wisdom and realization comes through spiritual understanding.

Wisdom

That the God of our Lord Jesus Christ, the Father of glory may give unto you the spirit of wisdom and revelation in the knowledge of Him.

Ephesians 1:17

God's Wisdom reveals, and then illuminates God's Will. In essence, God begins to make us aware of the plan and vision He has for our lives. He literally makes "The Master's Plan" understandable to us in our souls. The more we understand, the better we will be able to discern which decisions we should make. God's Wisdom causes us rightly to determine which is a God Idea and which is not.

God's Wisdom comes directly from the mind of God and is communicated to us through His Word—The Bible. When God's Wisdom is embedded in our hearts, minds and souls, it teaches and instructs us on what we should do and which way we should go. Proverbs 8:2-3 says, *"She standeth in the top of high places, by the way in the places of the paths. She crieth at the gates, at the entry of the city at the coming in at the doors."* In other words, God's Wisdom helps us to get to the top, find the right path, enter in through the right gate of the right city, and find our way in through the right door.

In addition, God's Wisdom reveals who God is and it shows us what is excellent and right for our lives. Proverb 8:6 says, *"Hear; for I will speak of excellent things; and the opening of my lips shall be right things."* However, it is up to us to get this wisdom embedded deeply in our hearts, minds and souls so that we can come to understand what "The Master's Plan" is. This way, we can make the best decisions as well as get on the best path that will cause us to achieve the best possible results in our lives.

A "How To" Strategy

The LORD possessed me in the beginning of his way, before his works of old. I was set up from everlasting, from the beginning, or ever the earth was.

Proverbs 8:22-23

God's Wisdom also provides us with a how to strategy. In the very beginning, God possessed this brand of wisdom, and with it, He knew how to put this whole thing together. He knew how to measure depths, settle mountains, prepare the heavens, establish the clouds, and decree the sea. Thus, with God's Wisdom we can learn how to make Godly decisions, how to get Godly results, how to overcome procrastination God's way, and how to live a life of no lack.

The beauty of all of this is, if we truly want to receive this how-to strategy with God's Wisdom, we should embed The Word in our hearts. At the same time, we should just ask God for it and He will give it to us. James 1:5 (NIV) says, *"If any of you lacks wisdom, he should ask God, who gives generously to all without finding fault, and it will be given to him."* However, if we do not do these things, we will continue to procrastinate because we will put off the fulfillment of our true potential.

Spiritual Understanding

And I filled him with the Spirit of God, in wisdom,
and in understanding, and in the knowledge,
and in all manner of workmanship.

Exodus 31:3

In the Hebrew, understanding is defined as: to distinguish; weigh as with scales; to ponder; or to grasp. Spiritual understanding enlightens our minds (illuminates; gives the light of knowledge of God's will) and enables us to grasp the fullness of what God is saying and doing in our lives. Also, it enables us to fully grasp how to overcome procrastination God's way, how to break the back of slack, and how to enter into the land of no lack.

We obtain Spiritual Understanding through the Holy Spirit who communicates and illuminates the message of God's Wisdom (The Word) embedded in our hearts, to our minds. In fact, the Holy Spirit is the Spirit of Wisdom, Revelation and Knowledge. That's why in Ephesians 1:17, Paul prayed that God would give *"the Spirit of wisdom and revelation in the knowledge of Him."* He did so because he knew that when our Spiritual understanding becomes enlightened (illuminated), we become empowered to make God decisions which are the best decisions any of us could make.

However, Spiritual Understanding is effective only to the extent to which God's Wisdom (God's Word) is embedded in our hearts. Psalm 119:130 says, *"The entrance of thy words giveth light, it giveth understanding unto the simple."* Thus, without the entrance of The Word into our hearts, the Holy Spirit does not have much "God Stuff" to work with. Therefore, we go spiritually un-enlightened and misinformed and as a result we make decisions based solely on what we perceive. That is never good because misperception becomes our reality and it opens the door to pseudo (false) realities such as fear, worry and shame. Once those things creep in, they loom underneath and become the most common underlying spiritual root causes of procrastination.

Summary of Knowledge, Wisdom and Spiritual Understanding

Knowledge of God's Will is obtained through establishing a relationship with The Lord Jesus Christ. He lives in our souls by way of the Holy Spirit. God's Wisdom dwells in our hearts by way of God's Word where it reveals the Mind of God. The Holy Spirit communicates the message of God's Wisdom to our minds and empowers us fully to comprehend (realize in our minds) God's Wisdom. With knowledge of God's Will, God's Wisdom, and Spiritual

Understanding, we become enabled to make God decisions which lead to the best results.

Without knowledge of God's Will, Wisdom and Spiritual Understanding, at best, we are left to our own perception of which decisions we should make or what routes we should take. The self-perceived road is often the road many people choose because it is the natural thing to do. However, our reliance on self-perception is not the best route because fear, worry and shame live there. Those three things are the most common underlying spiritual root causes of procrastination.

Diagram 1: Summary of Knowledge

	Where Found	How Established	What Happens
Knowledge of God's Will	Soul	Relationship with The Lord Jesus Christ	**Relates** us to God
God's Wisdom	Heart	God's Word	**Reveals** the mind and will of God
Spiritual Understanding	Mind	The Holy Spirit	We **Realize** the relationship and revelation of God

Prayer:

Father, I realize that I cannot make the best decisions without Knowledge of Your Will, Your Wisdom and Spiritual Understanding. I invite You to flood my heart, mind and soul with Your Presence so that I may be able to grasp Your perfect will for my life and be able to overcome the procrastination that stems from making bad decisions or no decisions at all. In Jesus' Name, I pray, Amen!

Summary of Scriptures:

Joel 3:14
Hosea 6:3
Proverb 21:10
Proverb 24:14
Proverb 19:2
Ecclesiastes 11:4
Matthew 11:27 (AMP)
Hebrews 11:6
Ephesians 1:17
Proverbs 8:2-3
Proverb 8:6
Proverbs 8:22-23
James 1:5 (NIV)
Exodus 31:3
Psalm 119:130

†

Chapter Four
Fear, Worry and Shame

Fear

Terrors are turned upon me: they pursue my soul as the wind:and my welfare passeth away as a cloud.

Job 30:15

One of the main underlying spiritual root causes of procrastination is fear. Suddenly, it enters in like a lion and dispenses distress, anguish and torment to our souls.

Our souls become torn by fear like lions tear at their prey. In Psalm 57:4, King David said, *"his soul was among lions."* The ultimate goal of fear is to persecute and paralyze our souls. If our souls are paralyzed, then we become disabled from going forward toward what God has ordained for our lives. Instead, with fear, we continue to procrastinate and experience lack in some area of our lives.

Also, fear distorts reality. The true reality is, God intends for us all to live no lack lives. In John 10:10 The Lord Jesus Christ says, *"I am come that they may have life and have it more abundantly."* Knowledge of God's Will, God's Wisdom and Spiritual Understanding gets us there. However, when we make decisions based on our own perception of reality, the enemy subtly introduces the counterfeit reality of fear and then slowly but surely begins to rob us of the no lack life that God intends. John 10:10 also says, *"The thief cometh not, but for to kill, steal and destroy."* He intends to kill, steal and destroy everything that God intends for our lives. Actually, the enemy does not have to do much because once we internalize fear we ultimately destroy ourselves. We procrastinate on taking the necessary steps that lead us to the land of no lack because we perceive that taking a step will be painful in some way.

For example, with the fear of failure or rejection, we are mainly afraid of the perceived pain that we will endure if we take a step. We procrastinate on going forward because we are either unsure of our abilities, or we loathe the embarrassment or ridicule we may face if we fail or if we are rejected.

With the fear of success, we procrastinate because of the perceived pain or embarrassment that may come from not knowing how to handle success, especially if we have never achieved that level of success before. Thus, because of fear, we don't go forward. Instead, we deliberate and procrastinate mainly because we do not want to experience pain.

Simply put, self perception opens up the entryway for fear to creep in and loom underneath. It then produces the false perception that going forward is going to hurt. Since we have experienced pain before, we procrastinate because we do not want to experience it ever again.

However, instead of avoiding pain, fear causes us to endure more pain, anguish, and torment because we end up thinking long and wrong on false evidence that appears to be real (F.E.A.R.). In other words, our fear-based misperceptions cause us to procrastinate because we spend so much time deliberating false realities instead of making the God decisions which ultimately will lead us to the land of no lack. That hurts! Publius Syrus, a first century writer said, "Opportunity often slips away because we deliberate on it." Ultimately, because of fear, we stop living and we end up just existing. Og Mandino said,"To be always intending to make a new and better life but never to find time to set about it is as...to put off eating and drinking and sleeping from one day to the next until you're dead." This is unacceptable.

Worry

The slothful man saith, there is a lion outside,
I shall be slain in the streets.

Proverb 22:13

Once fear deeply sets into our souls, it perpetuates itself through worry in our minds. It becomes the mechanism through which fear constantly attempts to convince us that we are powerless over our circumstances. In the case of worry, we are completely bound by our own perception of things and as a result, we procrastinate.

In Webster's Dictionary, worry is defined as: to be choked or strangled; or to be harassed by tearing, biting or snapping at the throat. This definition is very interesting because that is exactly how a lion kills its prey. Lions lie in wait until they detect weakness in their prey. Then they pounce upon it by grabbing it by the neck. They worry their prey to death. In other words, lions choke the very life out of their prey; sometimes slowly but always painfully.

In Proverb 22:13, *"The slothful man saith, there is a lion outside, I shall be slain in the streets."* Apparently, the man was slothful because he was worried that he would be eaten alive if he took a step outside. However, there is no real evidence that lions were waiting outside. Instead, it is possible that the man was simply verbalizing the worry that was matriculating through his mind.

He seemed to be saying, "what if" I take a step beyond where I am right now? I "probably will" experience some great measure of pain if I do. In other words, the man was being mentally harassed by his own self perception of what the end result was going to be. As a result, the man procrastinated because of something that did not exist.

In essence, the enemy infused fear into the man's soul and worry into the man's mind. Then, he pressed the "auto replay" button. As a result, the man became wound and bound by his own thoughts and ended up staying right where he was.The enemy does the same thing to us and we usually respond the same way. We too end up living life in the "what if" zone.

Because we spend so much time worrying about outcomes that are not supported by any real evidence and usually don't exist at all, we end up procrastinating on taking the necessary steps that will lead us to the land of no lack. For instance, I imagine that many people probably spend about 40% of every minute (24 of every 60 seconds or more) worrying about one thing or another. That means, if someone is 40 years old, and if 40% of life has been spent worrying, then that means 16 of their 40 years of life has been lost to worry. That means every second, minute and hour of every day for 16 years has been spent worrying about something that does not even exist. However, imagine if all of that time and energy could have been used to take more productive steps. We would be able to break the back of slack and enter into the land of no lack.

At best, worry constantly gnaws away at our throats, distracts us and causes us to procrastinate on taking possession of what is rightfully ours. At worst, worry can lead to all kinds of ailments which literally can kill us. Because of the state of indecision and inaction that fear and worry cause, we can also begin to experience other forms of perception-based drama which causes us to procrastinate even more.

Shame

Thou hast known my reproach, and my shame,
and my dishonour: mine adversaries are all before thee.
Reproach hath broken my heart; and I am full of heaviness:
and I looked for some to take pity, but there was none;
and for comforters, but I found none.

Psalm 69:19-20

When fear and worry cause us to procrastinate, we do not do what we desire to do, or we do not complete what we have already begun. As a result, we add insult to injury and we are often put to shame. We get double for our trouble and I don't mean that positively. Shame becomes a negative, after-the-fact consequence. Winston Churchill, the World War II-Era British Prime Minister, once said, "The era of procrastination, of half-measures, of soothing and baffling expedients, of delays, is coming to a close. In its place we are entering a period of consequences." One main consequence of procrastination is shame.

According to Proverb 10:5, *"He that gathereth in the summer is a wise son: but he that sleepeth in harvest is a son that causeth shame."* In essence, our struggle to go forward becomes more and more difficult because shame forces us to contend with yet another level of stuff that looms underneath and causes us to procrastinate even more. However, shame is an after-the-fact root cause. Shame is an internal reaction that we experience after we have not done something we were supposed to do; done something we were not supposed to do; or not completed something that we have begun. It's that ugghhh!!! feeling that we feel after the fact. In the Hebrew, shame has several related definitions. It means: *to be disappointed or delayed; confused; wounded, taunted, or insulted internally*. It also means: *to be held in self contempt or disgrace.* Hence, after we have made a bad decision or no decision, or after we have not completed something we desire or already started, we begin to hold ourselves in contempt and we find ourselves confused, wounded and taunted by that ugghh feeling that looms underneath.

For example, if we have not managed our money well and at the same time we have an obligation to pay a bill that we have not paid, then we are put to shame when we wrongly decide to procrastinate on taking action. Shame taunts us afterwards and makes it even more difficult to answer the telephone when the bill collector calls the next time. Or, if the bill collector sends us a letter or a bill, because we are ashamed, we do not open the letter. Then, the color of the envelope changes and the letter takes on a more adversarial and threatening tone. Or, when the bill collector leaves a message, it is a more irritated and nasty tone. Initially, we were afraid or worried, and then we were put to shame. All of that stuff looms underneath and causes further delay in our lives. Each round goes lower and lower. Depression sets in and we end up in bondage because we begin to feel like there is no way out of our situation.

We end up subjecting ourselves to more pain and expense than necessary and the enemy—the persecutor of souls—wins yet another battle. His goal is to get us to feel bad about ourselves and to get us to wallow in despair and reproach. In Psalm 69:19-20 King David said, *"Mine adversaries are all before thee. Reproach hath broken my heart; and I am full of heaviness: and I looked for some to take pity, but there was none; and for comforters, but I found none."* Doesn't that sound like bondage to you? Well, that's exactly what it is. Remember, all of this happens when we let fear and worry team up with shame in order to bring us to the point of despair. That is not good but it is not impossible to overcome. Whatever we did or did not do yesterday or the day before, we can confront and overcome it because today is a new day.

We are armed with a "how to" strategy provided by knowledge of God's will, Godly Wisdom and Spiritual Understanding. Therefore, with all of that fire power, we can make one of the best decisions we could ever make. We can decide to confront the fear, worry and shame or anything else that looms underneath and causes us to procrastinate in our lives. We should make this decision because too many of us have been in despair for far too long. At the same time, we cannot continue to avoid these issues because if we do, we will continue to be slack and lack in some area of our lives. That is not good because that is not what God intends for our lives.

Let me ask you…

Food For Thought

- **What's looming underneath and what is causing you to pause on making a decision to go forward in your life?**
- **Is it fear, worry or shame?**
- **Is your soul dwelling with the lions that constantly roar and cause your life to be at a standstill?**
- **Is your progress being hindered in going forward toward a life of no lack which includes peace of mind? If so, there is still good news; fear, worry and shame can be overcome with a confrontation.**

Prayer:

Father, I thank you that You have not given me the spirit of fear, but power, love and a sound mind. Therefore, In Jesus' Name, I lay an axe to the root of the fear, worry or shame that has caused me to procrastinate in my life and I take authority over every hindering spirit that has caused me to live in the spirit of bondage and lack in my life. In Jesus Name, I pray, Amen!

Summary of Scriptures:

Job 30:15

Psalm 57:4

John 10:10

Proverb 22:13

Psalm 69:19-20

Proverb 10:5

†

Chapter Five
Confrontation

The sluggard will not plow by reason of the cold;
therefore shall he beg in harvest, and have nothing.

Proverb 20:4

The underlying spiritual root causes of procrastination cause us to avoid doing things that we perceive will hurt, consume time and energy or are difficult or unpleasant. Therefore, it is necessary to investigate what happens when we do that. At the same time, we will learn that there are some supernatural strategies that we can employ in order to help us to confront and ultimately overcome the things that loom underneath and cause us to procrastinate.

First things first—avoidance causes things to get worse. For example, in Proverb 20:4, the sluggard man's situation got worse because he avoided taking care of some important business. It says, *"The sluggard will not plow by reason of the cold; therefore shall he beg in harvest, and have nothing."* In other words, he had to endure far more hardship and difficulty than was necessary. Had he gotten up, put on his boots and gloves and plowed his field, even in the midst of cold and harsh weather, he would have experienced a harvest in its due season. However, because he avoided taking action when he was supposed to, he had to beg when it came time for harvest and ultimately ended up with nothing. At first, taking care of business was a necessary evil, then, after he avoided taking care of business, he ended up enduring an evil that wasn't necessary.

The same thing happens to us. One thing leads to another. When we avoid confronting what needs to be confronted, our situations almost always get worse. We end up having to pay or do more than necessary; we almost always end up completely stressed out; and the overall quality of life diminishes. In Proverbs 24:30-31 (NIV), King Solomon said, *"I went past the field of the sluggard, past the vineyard of the man who lacks judgment; thorns had come up everywhere, the ground was covered with weeds, and the stone wall was in ruins."* He also said in Ecclesiastes 10:18, *"By much slothfulness the building decayeth; and through idleness of the hands the house droppeth through."*

Does any of this seem familiar? Have you ever needed to confront something or someone that was not pleasant, but because you didn't confront it, things got worse? Well, if we take the same course of action that the sluggard man took, then we will end up living in slack and lack in some area of our lives. Therefore, the question becomes, what are we going to do about it? Are we going to continue to avoid what needs to be confronted or are we going to confront what we have been avoiding? The former will yield unnecessary consequences but the latter will yield rewards. The choice is left up to us. The best choice is to take action by confronting whatever stands before us or in us.

Fear, worry and shame can be confronted and overcome. To confront something means we must be willing to come face to face with whatever we are dealing with, with an unquenchable determination to overcome it. The good news is we do not have to confront those things alone. God is with us.

The Big Show Down

For by thee I have run through a troop;
and by my God have I leaped over a wall.

Psalm 18:29

As we commence our journey to the land of no lack, we must confront the lions that loom and roar underneath in our hearts, minds and souls and cause us to procrastinate. By confronting the internal things, we will be empowered to confront the external things. However, confrontation is not easy because we are forced to approach those things that we either dread or those things that we perceive are more powerful than we are. Nevertheless, we should be encouraged because, with God's help, we can confront and overcome whatever needs to be confronted. Therefore, we must be willing to trust that God is able to defeat whatever is roaring on the inside and whatever is standing before us on the outside.

In Psalm 18:29, King David had some gigantic challenges that he had to confront. In that passage, he said, *"For by thee I have run through a troop; and by my God have I leaped over a wall."* In other words, David knew that because he had a close and personal relationship with God, He would help him to confront the fear, worry and shame that roared deep down inside as well as the difficult things he had to confront on the outside. As a result of David's faith, God empowered him to run through the troops and leap over the walls that stood before him. The good news is, the same God that King David knew, is the same God that we know. God will do for us what He did for David. He will bring us through whatever we are forced to face. With our God, we will be able to overcome the things that loom and roar inside of us as well as the things that stand before us. God is with us.

We should expect something good to happen as we take steps to overcome procrastination, break the back of slack and enter into the land of no lack. We should have complete confidence that we will emerge victorious no matter what when we confront fear, worry and shame with God's help. As we go forward, just know that we can overcome anything that stands in our in our way. However, we have to decide to confront whatever we are forced to face.

Confront The Lions of Fear & Worry

By the blast of God they perish,
and by the breath of His anger they are consumed.
The roaring of the lion, the voice of the fierce lion, and the teeth of the young lions are broken. The old lion perishes for lack of prey, and the cubs of the lioness are scattered.

Job 4:9-11 (NKJV)

God is well aware of the internal and external lions that loom and roar and cause us to procrastinate in our lives. At the same time, He wants us to be absolutely confident that there is nothing that can withstand the blast of His power. That includes the lions of fear, worry and shame. However, God is just waiting for us to decide, once and for all, to confront those things so that He can show us just how able and powerful He is. When we step to Him with faith, like David did, He will help us to run through troops and leap over walls. In other words, He will be with us and will help us to confront and overcome whatever we need to confront.

Believe & Pray

My God hath sent forth his angel, and hath shut the lions' mouths, that they have not hurt me...
So Daniel was taken up out of the den, and no manner of hurt was found upon him, because he believed in his God.

Daniel 6:22-23

In order to activate the power to confront the lions that roar in our lives, we simply need to believe. Belief in this context is defined in the Hebrew as: to be permanently true and certain; firm; and to go to the right hand. When Daniel was thrown into the lions' den that had been sealed shut with a stone, he had no where to run and no where to hide. Therefore, he had to make a conscious but quick choice to either be afraid or believe that God was going to get him out of the situation that he was in. Daniel chose to believe and was absolutely certain that God was going to deliver him out of the mouths of the lions. That's exactly what God did. God delivered him because he believed and because he prayed.

Belief is the foundation upon which answered prayer is built. We believe and then we pray. As a result, God answers our prayers because we believe. That's what Daniel did. Daniel was unshakably certain that God would deliver him out of the mouths of the lions because he lived a lifestyle of prayer. In fact, the reason why he was thrown into the lions' den in the first place was because he was found on his knees praying when prayer had been forbidden. However, Daniel didn't care because he continuously believed and prayed to God. He believed that since God had helped him before, He would help him again.

Do you think Daniel shook in his boots with paralyzing fear or do you think he prayed while he was in the lions' den? I believe he prayed because otherwise he would have been eaten alive. Remember, lions specialize in devouring prey that are too paralyzed with fear to escape. Thus, Daniel must have taken a different course of action. Daniel 6:23 exclaims that he *"was taken up out of the den, and no manner of hurt was found upon him, because he believed in his God."* This was the case because Daniel believed and prayed. Therefore, God released His power and shut the mouths of the lions so that they could not harm him. What God did for Daniel, He will do for us.

God is just waiting for us to do what Daniel did—live a lifestyle of belief and prayer. In turn, God will activate His power and will shut the mouths of the lions of fear, worry, and shame that loom underneath and cause us to procrastinate. Job 4:9-11 says, *"By the blast of God they perish, and by the breath of His anger they are consumed. The roaring of the lion, the voice of the fierce lion, and the teeth of the young lions are broken. The old lion perishes for lack of prey, and the cubs of the lioness are scattered."* When we believe this by faith, God will show up at the appointed time and in a powerful way.

God will unleash His mighty power in us and will give us the courage to confront and defeat whatever needs to be confronted. Imagine if the slothful man in Proverb 22:13 would have been aware that God was with Him, He never would have been worried or afraid and never would have said, *"There is a lion outside, I shall be slain in the streets."* Instead, he would have confronted whatever he was worried about or afraid of and would have taken a step towards living the no lack life that God had planned for his life.

We should learn a thing or two from him. We don't have to be stifled by the perceived or real fear of any lion that is roaring internally or externally in our lives. Therefore, we should not waste any more time asking what if? Instead, we should confront the lions with the power that comes from God. We've got the Power! We can activate it with our belief that God is with us and in us and that He will answer our prayers.

Take a moment and ask yourself:

Food For Thought

- **Are any lions of fear and worry roaring on the inside of me? If so, what is my course of action?**
- **Do I believe and pray that God is going to shut the mouths of the lions that loom and roar underneath? Or do I continue to avoid taking action?**

Please choose wisely because overcoming procrastination depends on whether we confront whatever needs to be confronted internally and externally.

The Confrontation of Shame

There is therefore now no condemnation to them
which are in Christ Jesus
who walk not after the flesh, but after the Spirit.

Romans 8:1

As we have already learned, shame causes us to be disappointed or delayed, confused, wounded, taunted or insulted internally and we find ourselves condemned because we did something that we were not supposed to do, or we did not do something that we were supposed to do. Either way, continually we contemplate what happened in the past, and as a result, we put off living in the present and the future. We procrastinate even more. However, there are at least two ways that we can overcome shame and therefore be released from the extra layer of bondage that it brings. In order to confront and overcome shame we should live in the here and now, and we should walk in the Spirit.

- **Live in the Here and Now**
- **Walk in the Spirit**

Live in The Here and Now

There is therefore now no condemnation to them which are in Christ Jesus.

Romans 8:1

To live in the here and now means we live in the present and not the past. However, if we continue to recount, over and over, what we should or should not have done, then our focus can only be on the past. Under those circumstances, the roar of shame will eat us alive mentally, spiritually, and physically. As a result, we will end up procrastinating in some way or another. At best, our progress will be stifled or at worst, our lives will be brought to a screeching halt. Therefore, it is not healthy to stay in a perpetual state of shame and condemnation over the infractions or inactions of the past. Instead, we should shift our focus away from what we did or didn't do, to what our next steps are going to be.

However, this process is difficult because the enemy vigorously roars and fights with everything he has in order to kill, steal and destroy the no lack life that God has made available to us before it ever comes to pass. He roars and fights from the lion's den of shame. What better strategy than to continuously remind us of what we have or haven't done? With shame we remain distracted, in despair, and in disgrace and as a result, we waste time and energy. We procrastinate on entering into the land of no lack.

To live in perpetual shame is a tragedy because shame and condemnation have already been defeated. Revelation 12:10 tells us that *"The accuser of our brethren is cast down which accused them before our God day and night."* That means the accusers' accusations and condemnations that cause us to walk in shame, and cause us to procrastinate have already been defeated by the power of Christ, Who came to set us free from bondage. As a result, there is therefore now no condemnation (or shame) to them who are in Christ.

In other words, when The Lord Jesus Christ died on the cross, the power of His blood that was shed was and still is more powerful than the bondage of sin and shame. His death and resurrection from the dead created a new atmosphere of life that lacks nothing for those who believe. Thus, to live in the here and now means that we live in Christ and Christ lives in us. As a result, we are able to live in the new reality of freedom that He created for us. We are also able to have a new Godly perspective on how we can exit the past and enter into the future unfettered by the constant nagging and taunting that shame brings.

Similarly, to live in the here and now by living in Christ means that we live in the fullness of life that God has provided. Colossians 2:9-10 (NKJV) states, *"For in Him dwells all the fullness of the Godhead bodily;*

and you are complete in Him, who is the head of all principality and power." This means that when we allow God to be in control of every area, our lives will be complete and full in every way. There is no place for shame because shame attempts to convince us that somehow we are incomplete in some way. Therefore, we should live free from shame and condemnation, and we should live in the fullness that God provides. Hallelujah! We're free! But, there is a but.

Walk After The Spirit

Walk not after the flesh, but after the Spirit.

Romans 8:1

As we live freely in the here and the now, in Christ, we must also maintain our freedom by walking after the Spirit. That means that we will be able to victoriously trample over whatever stands before us or in us. That includes: fear, worry and shame and anything else that causes us to procrastinate.

Walking after the Spirit also means that we are on the move, but not by ourselves. Instead, we walk with complete confidence that God's Spirit is with us and in us. Therefore, when we move, He leads while we follow. When we follow closely, shame has no room to taunt us or tear at our souls. However, if we chose not to walk after the Spirit, we end up walking in the flesh which dilutes the potency of God's Spirit operating in us. As a result, we feel like we are walking by ourselves. At least, that is what the accuser of the brethren wants us to believe. However, there is nothing farther from the truth. No matter what the enemy tries to get us to buy into, if we have the Holy Spirit living on the inside of us, then all of God lives on the inside of us. That means God is with us even when we are forced to confront something that looms and roars deep down inside and causes us to procrastinate in our lives.

Therefore, what are we concerned, afraid or ashamed about? What is looming underneath and is causing us to be slack, sluggish or slothful in going forward toward the attainment of the life of no lack that God has planned? What's causing us to procrastinate? What needs to be confronted? Whatever it is, just remember there is nothing too hard for God!

Practical Steps That Can Be Taken To Confront Whatever is Standing Your Way

STEP 1: Make a list of the unpleasant or difficult things, situations or people that need to be confronted. *(See The Confrontation Chart Diagram 2 on page 55).*

For example:

- ☐ Pay past due bills and debts
- ☐ Satisfy IRS obligations
- ☐ Check credit score and repair credit
- ☐ Forgive someone who needs to be forgiven
- ☐ Contact a child, family member, or friend that you've been avoiding because you've either hurt or disappointed them or you have been hurt or disappointed by them
- ☐ Set a doctor or dentist appointment that you've been avoiding
- ☐ Lose weight
- ☐ Go back to school
- ☐ De-clutterize clutter
- ☐ Open up unopened mail or answer unanswered emails
- ☐ ________________________________

STEP 2: Determine the Cause of Avoidance.

- Ask yourself: *Why am I avoiding (not confronting) taking action on these things? Is it because of fear, worry, shame or something else?*

- Write down your answer.

STEP 3: Match up the unpleasant or difficult thing(s) that you have written down with an emancipating scripture that addresses the thing(s) that you are avoiding.

- This will build up your faith and your confidence so that you can boldly confront whatever needs to be confronted.

STEP 4: Approach God with your concern with confidence in knowing that He is able and willing to help you to confront what needs to be confronted.

- God is with you and in you. In other words, pray about it like Daniel did when he was in the lions' den.
- Take spiritual authority over whatever is causing you to procrastinate. Whatever it is, it cannot withstand the blast from God.

STEP 5: Ask God for knowledge, wisdom and spiritual understanding in knowing how and when to confront whatever needs to be confronted.

STEP 6: Confront it (take action) like Samson did with the power of The Holy Spirit living on the inside of you.

Diagram 2: Confrontation Table

Things Avodied	Cause of Avoidance	Emancipating Scripture	Course of Action	Completion Date

(Download Form at www.The777Plan.com)

"At that moment the Spirit of the LORD came powerfully upon him, and he ripped the lion's jaws apart with his bare hands. He did it as easily as if it were a young goat..."

Judges 14:5-6 NLT

Prayer:

Father, I need your help! There are some things that I have been avoiding because I am afraid or worried or wrought with shame about what the outcome or report is going to be. I know You have not given me the spirit of fear, but power, love and a sound mind. Your Word promises that You would help me to leap over walls and run through hostile troops. So, Father, please help me to confront whatever needs to be confronted on the inside or on the outside. In The Name of The Lord Jesus Christ, I pray, Amen!

Summary of Scriptures:

Proverb 20:4

Proverbs 24:30-31

Ecclesiastes 10:18

Psalm 18:29

Job 4:9-11 (NKJV)

Daniel 6:22-23

Proverb 22:13

Romans 8:1

Revelation 12:10

Colossians 2:9-10 (NKJV)

Judges 14:5-6 (NLT)

†

Part II

A Practical Guide to Dig Out from The Past, Manage The Present, & Enter Into The Future

As we learned in Part I, the seven procrastinating tribes may have been slack, sluggish or slothful to leave Shiloh and enter into the land of no lack because they may not have had vision or may not have been able to make God decisions. Or, they may have allowed the lions of fear, worry or shame to loom underneath in their hearts, minds or souls without confronting those things. At the same time, it is possible that they may have opted to stay at Shiloh because they may not have known how to strategically put things in order so that they could effectively and efficiently make a move. That is the case for many of us. We procrastinate because we simply don't know what to do.

Since we've been at Shiloh for so long, we don't know how to live our lives any differently. We have opted to live in that place of comfortable discomfort and have acquiesced to live life by default. This is so because we do not know how to gain order. Some of us have spent a lot of time and money and have tried elaborate plans and systems but we still do not have order. As a result, many of us have returned right back to Shiloh for another season of living in lack and slack. We must find a way to strategically plan our lives and to diligently implement that plan so that we can leave Shiloh once and for all.

When Joshua noticed that the seven remaining tribes were slack to take a step, he suggested a strategy which helped them to put things together and get them moving out of Shiloh and into the land of no lack. It worked for them and I believe that we can tailor it to work for us in the 21st Century. There are some practical steps we can take to dig out from the past, manage the present, and enter into the future.

Chapter Six
Order

Let all things be done decently and in order.

1 Corinthians 14:40

The seven procrastinating tribes remained at Shiloh because they did not have a strategy to help them to gain, regain, or maintain order.

We know this because Joshua gave them specific instructions to describe and divide the land of no lack that had already been conquered for them. Those instructions to gain order were critical because he knew that without order, they would be forced to live beneath the standard of life that God had ordained for them. For example, Joshua must have known that having a lack of order would cause continued procrastination. That's why he asked them how long they were going to be slack to go and possess. Then, he developed a strategy to get them moving. We are no different. Without order in our lives, we too will procrastinate and our affairs will continue to back up and stack up against us. Therefore, we too need a strategy to gain order so that we can get moving towards the land of no lack.

Lack of order may be a result of a lack of regimentation or discipline early in life, or it may be the result of some extraordinary event such as the birth of a child, the death of a loved one, marriage or divorce, the gain or loss of a job, or some other life changing event. Either way, many of us suffer because we want to get things done but without order, we can't.

Therefore, we must take action. We must develop a strategy that will help us gain order so that we can dig out from the past, manage the present, and enter into a no lack future. In order to do this, we should do the following:

- **Understand What Order Is**
- **Determine What Needs To Be Dug Out From the Past**
- **Determine What Needs To Be Done Right Now**
- **Determine What Desires To Accomplish in the Future**

Understand What Order Is

To every thing there is a season,
and a time to every purpose under the heaven

Ecclesiastes 3:1

Order is a system that organizes and places everything in its proper place and enables everything to function properly. Also, with order we operate effectively and efficiently and we accomplish our desires. Order is the mechanism through which God accomplishes what He desires for our lives.

God's Original Strategy to Gain Order

In the beginning God created the heaven and the earth.
And the earth was without form, and void;
and darkness was upon the face of the deep.
And the Spirit of God moved upon the face of the waters.
And God said, Let there be light: and there was light.

Genesis 1:1-3

Genesis 1:1-3 is the very first lesson in the Bible and it is a lesson on gaining order. In the beginning when God created heaven and earth, it was void and without form. Darkness was upon the face of the deep. Then, the Spirit of God moved and God said let there be... and there was order! It was a six day process of creating a system where darkness became light, timelessness became measured in increments of night and day, time and seasons, and barrenness became fruitfulness.

God could have blinked, and it all could have been done in a flash.

Instead, He walked us all the way through the process so that we could gain insight into what it takes to transform chaos into order. It is a process. Nevertheless, God did not indicate that going through the process would be quick or easy. Perhaps, that is why He rested on the seventh day. Indeed, gaining order can be quite grueling especially if we have always lived disorderly lives. However, it is worth it to go through the process because order makes life so much easier to manage.

Gaining, regaining and maintaining order requires a strategy and endurance. Without a strategy, we will most likely give it a try one more time, for a little while, but then go right back to living disorderly lives. Therefore, our strategy to gain, regain and maintain order *(put everything in its proper place, time and season)* requires that we:

- **Determine what our past due, unfulfilled obligations are**
- **Take inventory of our current obligations**
- **Consider what we desire to accomplish in the future**

Determine What Needs To Be Dug Out From the Past—*Can You Dig It?*

Doesn't "digging out" sound like drudgery? It may, because it sounds like a lot of back-breaking work. But if we look a little closer, digging out is not so bad after all because it helps us to clear away all of that stuff that has stacked up against us. It also clears space in our minds for more positive thoughts. If we don't dig out, then all of those unfulfilled desires and obligations will continue be unfulfilled, and they will continue to haunt us and gnaw at our peace of mind.

The choice is left up to us. We can invoke the "ostrich method" which means we hide our heads in the sand and pretend our past due obligations don't exist. Or, we can choose to do the deep digging and heavy lifting that will help us to overcome procrastination God's way, break the back of slack, and ultimately enter into the land of no lack.

Can you dig it? Sure you can. This is how: Jot down a quick list of all of your past due unfulfilled obligations in every area of your life. This may take some time because you may have to dredge up some things that have been buried under in your mind. If possible, give it a shot because doing so will help you to unravel that stuff that has been weighing you down. *(See Diagram 3 on the next page).*

Diagram 3: Obligations

Past Due Obligations	Current Obligations	Future Pursuits

(Download Form at www.The777Plan.com)

Determine What Needs To Be Done Right Now–*Manage the Present*

Wouldn't it be nice if we were able to manage all of our current obligations so that everything is current and up to date? I am sure your answer would be a resounding *YES!* I know a few people who are able to timely manage all of their current obligations and I have often wondered what their secret is. I have discovered people like that live orderly lives. On the other hand, people who have challenges with managing the present usually live disorderly lives.

If you live a disorderly life, then your current obligations are probably difficult to manage. As a result, most likely, your current obligations have begun to morph into your already overwhelming stack of past due obligations. As a result, we end up living presently in the past. If you are shaking your head saying to yourself "yep, that's me," then fret not and neither let your heart be troubled because this monster can be slain. It is possible to dig out from the past, manage the present and enter into the future. Trust me, if I can slay this monster, then anybody can, so please be encouraged.

Okay then, what should we do? I suggest that you should quickly jot down a list of your current obligations *(See Diagram 3, at left).* These are things we are obligated to do either on an ongoing and recurring basis or just once or immediately. To help get you started, you might have some current obligations in the following areas: church or community, house or home, family, spiritual, personal or financial life, or work or school.

Also, another way to manage our current obligations is to start thinking about them differently. In other words, obligations are things that we have to do but thinking about them that way conjures stress. However, if we think about what we have to do as something that we want to do, then we will develop a desire to do what must be done. Most likely, we will accomplish what we want to accomplish instead of what we have to accomplish. So from now on, I'll refer to current obligations as current desires. Thus, let me ask you, what are your current desires in every area of your life? Jot them down but don't spend too much time here. We will use these data later.

Determine What Desires To Accomplish in the Future—*Enter into the Future*

As we've already discovered, our ultimate goal is to shift from living presently in the past to living presently, peacefully and progressively in the future. Reaching this point is sweet because those nagging unfulfilled obligations get fulfilled, current desires get managed well, and future desires get accomplished. According to Proverb 13:19, *"Desire accomplished is sweet to the soul."* You can make this shift. You can exit the past and enter into this sweet new future that is filled with accomplished desires. It all comes down to implementing a strategy that empowers us to accomplish them.

Let's think about the options for a minute. If we keep doing what we've always done, then we will get what we've always gotten. But, if we do something different, then we will get different and better results. I opt for the latter and pray that you do as well. Do you remember what you said your vision was for your life at the end of Chapter 2? If not, let me ask you again, what vision do you have for your life? What does a no lack life look like to you? What desires do you want to accomplish in your life? What do you want the present and your future to look like? Do you want to exit the past, enjoy the present and enter comfortably into the future? Of course you do.

I assure you that with a strategy, your past unfulfilled obligations and desires will get fulfilled, your current desires will be managed well, and your future desires will be accomplished. Most importantly, please keep in mind that this is what God desires for us. *"He will fulfill the desire of them that fear Him"* (Psalm 145:19) and *"The desire of the righteous shall be granted"* (Proverb 10:24). However, we've got to do our part. We must implement a strategy that invokes knowledge of God's will, Wisdom and Spiritual Understanding, and we must commit ourselves to see it through. We will exit the past and eventually we will enter into the future. Therefore, quickly jot down those things you want to accomplish in the future *(See, Diagram 3)*.

Now, all we need is a strategy to get all of these things working together for our good. Implementing the strategy will be filled with many challenges, especially in the beginning stages because literally it is a shift in the way we live our lives. It is also an ongoing process that must be assessed and reassessed because most assuredly our circumstances will change as life changes. Nonetheless, at some point, the paradigm will shift. The past will be just that–the past. The present will be enjoyed and simultaneously we'll begin to enter into a future that will be filled with accomplishments. Finally, a good strategy will help us to break the back of slack so that we can enter into the land of no lack.

Joshua's God Inspired Strategy– The 777 Plan™

The seven procrastinating tribes in Joshua 18:2-3 sat there idly and merely glanced at the land of no lack. They did not take a step. It was simple; they needed a strategy to help them to gain order and put things in proper perspective. In Joshua 18:3-6, Joshua devised a strategy to help them gain order so they could take possession of what was rightfully theirs. That same plan will help us to break the back of slack so we can enter into the land of no lack.

Prayer:

Father, please help me to gain, re-gain and maintain order in my life. There are some unfulfilled desires from the past, some current desires that need to be managed, and some future desires that I want to accomplish. However, I realize that I can do nothing without Your help. So, Father, help me to gain order so that Your perfect will can be performed in my life. In Jesus' Name, I pray, Amen!

Summary of Scriptures:

I Corinthians 14:40

Ecclesiastes 3:1

Psalm 145:19

Proverb 10:24

Joshua 18:2-6

Notes

†

Chapter Seven
The 777 Plan™

And Joshua said unto the children of Israel, How long are ye slack to go possess the land, which the Lord God of your fathers hath given you? Give out from among you three men for each tribe: and I will send them, and they shall rise, and go through the land, and describe it according to the inheritance of them; and they shall come again to me. And they shall divide it unto seven parts...

Ye shall therefore describe the land into seven parts, and bring the description hither to me, that I may cast lots for you here before the Lord your God.

Joshua 18:3-6.

- **7 Main Areas of Life's Desires** (assess the whole situation)
- **7 Actions** (break every area of desire down into manageable, achievable parts)
- **7 Months to Achieve** (take action by implementing the plan)

In Joshua 18, the seven procrastinating tribes were slack, slothful, and sluggish in taking a step into the land of no lack because they lacked order.

Therefore, Joshua suggested that they assess the whole situation and then break it down into achievable, manageable parts. We should do likewise. We should consider Joshua's plan for the seven procrastinating tribes and implement it in our lives. In order to implement Joshua's 777 Plan™ we need to assess our lives as a whole and then break them down into achievable, manageable parts. If we follow these steps, it should take about seven months to start seeing some substantive results.

It took me about *seven months* to break some bad, old habits and to establish some new, good ones. And it took me about *two years* to reach the shifting point from living presently in the past to living presently, peacefully and progressively in the future. In fact, up to the time of the writing of this book, I am still working it out and will continue to follow the plan because I feel out of sorts when I don't. It has become a way of life for me and it has brought some structure and order to the way I do things. It works for me and I hope it works for you too.

Imagine living without the burden of the past constantly gnawing at your soul; where the present is being managed well; and there is a vigorous pursuit of the future. Sound good? It is possible. But, please know that getting our lives in order in this way can be a rather exhausting process and there are no short cuts. This process is a marathon and not a sprint. It requires some heavy lifting and relentless plowing. But know that the heavy lifting on the front end makes the load lighter and easier to carry down the road.

That might be difficult to process because our generation is the microwave generation. We want things done quickly and easily. We do not want to work slowly through a painful process. You'll find, however, that working all the way through the process brings the best results. Nothing will be left undone. Old habits will get broken and new and better ways will be firmly established. Ultimately, our paradigms will shift from living presently in the past to living progressively and peacefully in the future.

If I can do it, anyone can! My life was so out of order I thought that it would be impossible to get out of the pit that I was in. It wasn't! My paradigm shifted and so will yours. Therefore, please be encouraged because God knows what we are going through and has given us a way to escape. He has given us a strategy to gain, regain and maintain order. Let's break it down.

In each of our lives, there are at least seven main areas that we must contend with simultaneously. Thus, in order for us to have order, balance and productivity in every area, we should consider the following strategy. There are:

- **7 Main Areas of Life Desires**
  (assess the whole situation)
- **7 Actions**
  (break every area of desire down into manageable, achievable parts)
- **7 Months to Achieve**
  (take action by implementing the plan)

7 Areas of Life Desires

You shall therefore describe the land into seven parts.

Joshua 18:6

Joshua instructed the seven procrastinating tribes to describe the land into seven parts so that each tribe could get a glimpse of what the entire lay of the land looked like. This was important because it changed the perception that moving forward would be so overwhelming. Once they knew what they were working with, all they had to do was break it down and achieve it. In the Hebrew, to describe means *to give an accounting of something.* Thus, if we adapt

Joshua's wisdom, we too will need to describe (give an account of) what we have going on in our lives. This means we should assess and identify every area of desire in our lives. If we don't assess the situation, then most likely we will stay right where we are. We will not enter into the land of no lack and everything will remain overlapped, convoluted and daunting: impossible to achieve.

However, taking this step is not that hard. It just requires that we identify the various areas of desire we have in our lives. In describing our overall situation, most people have at least seven (7) main areas of desire in their lives. The seven main areas of desire are:

- **Spiritual Desires:** devotion, prayer, worship (personal and corporate) Bible Study (personal and corporate), church obligations, participating in ministry, etc.;
- **Desires for House and Home:** having an orderly, organized and clean house etc.;
- **Personal Care Desires:** doctor and dentist visits, good diet, proper fitness, adequate rest and recreation, grooming, proper weight management, etc.;
- **Desires for Family and Friends:** spending quality time with and caring for family and friends,

getting and staying in touch with family and friends, mending fences with foes, etc.;

- **Financial Desires:** tithing, budgeting, payment of bills, mortgage or rent, savings, investment, repairing credit,eliminating debt, filing and paying taxes, etc.;
- **Work and/or School Desires:** meeting deadlines, projects, exams,assignments, etc.;
- **Desires for the Future:** fulfilling dreams and visions, embarking upon new ventures, starting or finishing school, etc.

The 7 main areas of desire in life listed above are not arranged in any specific order except the first area, Spiritual Desires, which should be first but is often the main area of procrastination in our lives. For most of us, we simply say, "I just don't have enough time or energy to pray, or read the Word of God." However, Mathew 6:33 says, *"Seek ye first the Kingdom of God and His righteousness, then all these things will be added unto us."* Therefore, by putting God first, we will have proper divine order and He will provide us with the necessary knowledge, wisdom and spiritual understanding we need to better manage every area of life.

Let me encourage you because this step is an easy one to take. This step entails a mere identification of the main areas of desire in our lives. You may discover that you have more than seven and if so, that's ok. But if you significantly have more than seven, then most likely you have too much going on. If that is the case, then perhaps the time has come to assess why you've got so much going on. It may also be time to determine what can be released, better prioritized, or delegated. At any rate, we should not spend too much time here because exercises like this give us a false sense of security. But, truth be told, we've only just begun. The heavy lifting is yet to follow.

What are the main areas of desire in your life? Describe (give an account of) them. Remember, most people have:

- ☐ Spiritual Desires
- ☐ Desires for House and Home
- ☐ Personal Care Desires
- ☐ Desires for Family and Friends
- ☐ Financial Desires
- ☐ Work and/or School Desires
- ☐ Desires for the Future
- ☐ ______________________
- ☐ ______________________
- ☐ ______________________

Do you have any additional areas of desire in your life? If so, include them on the list above. We will deal with this information shortly.

7 Actions

They shall divide it into seven portions.

Joshua 18:5

After we have identified the 7 main areas of desire in our lives, we will need to break those areas of desire down into the 7 portions (actions).

The Seven Actions Are the Following:

Divide each of the 7 Areas of Desire into 7 Actions:

(See Diagram 4, page 80)

- **Action 1:** Overall Tasks
- **Action 2:** Action Steps to Accomplish each Overall Task
- **Action 3:** Frequency of Action Steps
- **Action 4:** Completion of Action Steps
- **Action 5:** Cost of Actions (time or money)
- **Action 6:** Help in Taking or Completing Step
- **Action 7:** Plotting and Planning our Steps

We will need to complete this step for each of the seven (7) areas of desire. For example: Follow the same process for:

- **Spiritual Desires**
- **Desires for House and Home**
- **Personal Care Desires**
- **Desires for Family and Friends**
- **Financial Desires**
- **Desires for Work and/or School Desires**
- **Future Desires**
- **And other areas of desire that may be applicable to your life**

Action1: Overall Tasks

An overall task is a function that needs to be performed overall. For example, the far left column of Diagram 4 describes what the overall tasks are for the Desires for House and Home Area of Life. There are six overall tasks that need to be accomplished and they include: house cleaning, dry cleaning, clothes laundering, food shopping, car maintenance, and other special projects around the house. In order to gain or regain and maintain order in that area, I need to accomplish those overall tasks. To do that, I need to break those overall tasks down

Diagram 4: Area of Life Desires For House & Home

Overall Task/Project	Steps	Frequency	Completion Day/Date		Cost	Helps
House Cleaning	Vacuum	Weekly (W)	Sat		30 min	
	Scrub Bathroom	W	Sat		30 min	
	Mop Kitchen Floor	Bi-Weekly (Bi-W)	Sat		30 min	
	Wax Furniture & Wash Windows	Monthly (M) M	Sat		2 Hrs	
	Make Beds	Daily (D)	D		10 min	
	Wash Dishes	D	D		15 min	
	Declutter & Organize	Immediate(I) & Ongoing		End of Month	A While	
Dry Cleaning	Take Clothes to Cleaners	I & W	Mon			
Laundry	Wash Clothes	I & Bi-W	Fri			
Food Shopping	Go Food Shopping	I & Bi-W	Fri		$150	
	Get Toiletries	I & Bi-W	Fri		$50	
Car Maintenance	Change Oil	I & Quarterly		End of Month	$30	
	Get Gas	I & Bi-W	Sat		$200 mo	
	Get Car Detailed	I & Bi-W			$30 mo	
Special Projects Around the House	Clean Office Reorganize Files	I			1/2 day	
	Clean Off Back Porch	I			30 min	
	Remove Old Car Out back	I		By End of Month		

(Download Form at www.The777Plan.com)

into action steps. That will be covered in the next section. That's not too bad, right? I hope not. This step may take some time but not much.

Action 2: Action Steps to Accomplish Each Overall Task

Action steps for each overall task are the specific steps we take to accomplish or maintain each overall task for each area of life. Again, let's consult Diagram 4. The second column from the left provides examples of the specific action steps that need to be taken to accomplish each overall task. For example, in order to accomplish the overall task of cleaning house, I must take the following actions steps: vacuuming, scrubbing the bathroom, mopping the kitchen floor, waxing the furniture, and washing the windows etc... This is not too bad either, right? Again, I hope not. The hardest part about all of this is the time it takes to think through it. But, there's nothing hard about it at all. Again, let me remind you, this exercise needs to be completed for every overall task in each of the seven (or more) areas of life.

Action 3: Frequency of Action Steps for Each Overall Task

(How Often Each Action Step Needs To Be Performed)

Frequency of action steps determines how frequently we take the necessary action steps in order to accomplish each overall task in each area of life. Determining the frequency of the steps is very important because it helps us to sort out how often we do what we do. Again by consulting Diagram 4, we see that each specific step is taken either Daily (D), Weekly (W), Bi-weekly (BW), Monthly (M), Quarterly (Q), Bi-Annually (BA) or Annually (A). You may also notice that there are some steps that must be taken Immediately (I). Those things are usually past due or need some immediate attention or both. In addition, some action steps might be both immediate and ongoing. Those steps need to be done right now and need to be completed on an ongoing basis on Mondays. For example, Diagram 4 indicates that I need to take my clothes to the dry cleaners right now (*e.g.* my dry cleaning started to stack up on me)...I digress.

At any rate, in the future, I will need to continue taking my clothes to the dry cleaners on a weekly basis. Now, I can begin to bring order to my house and home and I will both fulfill a past due obligation (taking my dry cleaning to the cleaners immediately) and I will determine when and how often my dry cleaning will need to be taken to the cleaners (weekly). As a result, my dry cleaning will not stack up against me in the future and I have begun to dig out from the past, better manage the present, and enter into a more peaceful and orderly future in that area. Imagine if we could gain the same type of order in every area of life. Wouldn't that be awesome? Of course it would. It can be done.

Action 4: Completion Day or Date for Each Action Step

Now we are getting more specific. Here, our goal is to determine what day or date we desire to accomplish each specific action step for each overall task. Thinking through what day or date we do things helps us to focus on the specifics of when we will begin to turn our desires into accomplishments. Going through this part of the process causes our minds to shift away from defeat and delay, to action and accomplishment. However, it is important to remember that this is a marathon and not a sprint. It requires assessment and re-assessment as well as trial and error. But ultimately, we will begin to see the fruits of our labor.

Our paradigms will shift from living presently in the past to living peacefully and progressively in the future. Please trust me, as I was thinking, praying and living through this process, I went through trials, errors and frustrations. But, because I went through that, I came to understand that I had to keep plowing through even though it seemed like it was a bit much. I also found myself getting frustrated because, at first, I set unreasonable deadlines. Also, since I was the quintessential procrastinator, it was extremely difficult for me to stay focused. But, because I kept at it, past unfulfilled desires got fulfilled; present desires became easier to manage; and future desires got accomplished. One example is the completion of this book.

Specifically, if we consult Diagram 4 again, we will discover that each action step has a frequency and a completion day or date. For example, when I vacuum weekly, I do so on Saturday (or at least I desire to). By considering this, we're able to determine and re-determine specifically when we are going to take a step towards the accomplishment of our desires. Also, when we assess what days or dates we do things, we are able to determine if we have too much happening on certain days. If we do, then we can spread action steps out onto other days or dates. Doing this will bring balance and will help us to be better stewards over our time. In addition, we will be able to use this information when we start plotting (scheduling) our plans. This step will be tweaked as we go along, but we've got to start somewhere.

Action 5: Cost of Time or Money

Thinking through how much time or money it costs to complete certain steps serves a dual purpose. On the one hand, we begin to determine the actual or projected costs of time or money for each action step. On the other hand, we develop a budget/spending plan. I know budget/spending plan is a dirty word because most people don't use them. However, if we truly desire to overcome procrastination God's way, break the back of slack, and enter into a life of no lack, we will also need to get a grip on our finances. Thus, having a budget is extremely important.

Just think, we've already begun to confront something that is usually a grizzly bear to confront. When we go through this part of the process, we will be able to transfer the information from each area of life right onto whatever budget/spending plan sheet or process we choose to use. I am not suggesting that this will be easy but I am suggesting that it is necessary to a great degree. Also, when we determine how much time it takes to accomplish our action steps, we will be able to better budget our time. OK, now breathe in and breathe out. Let's move on.

Action 6: Help in Taking or Completing Steps

This section is not that deep but it is helpful. It simply helps us to think through what human or other resources are available to help us to accomplish our desires. I would not spend too much time here but it is worth it to think through it because we may actually find someone or something that can make it easier for us to dig out from the past, manage the present, and enter into the future.

Action 7: Plotting and Planning Our Steps

Plotting our steps involves grouping all of the like kind frequencies together. When we plot our action steps we will transfer all like kind frequencies from all of the 777 Plan™ worksheets from every area of life onto one 777 Plan™ Plotting Form *(See Diagram 5)*. We might have several pages of the same plotting form but we should use just one form. By plotting (grouping) our steps together, we will be able to determine:

- **What we have going on a recurring (ongoing) basis; and**
- **What we have to do immediately or just once.**

It is important to make this distinction because ongoing action steps become routine when we accomplish them over and over. When this happens, we will also be able to better identify available time slots to accomplish our immediate or one time action steps. As a result, we will be able to simultaneously dig out from the past and better manage the present. Ultimately, we will enter into a future that is unfettered with unfulfilled past due obligations.

Plotting: Grouping Like Frequencies Together

This is where we begin to shift our focus from identification to

Diagram 5: 777 Plan™ Plotting Form

Month						
One Time/ Immediate	Daily	Weekly/ Bi-Weekly	Monthly/ Bi-Monthly	Quarterly	Bi-Annually	Annually

(Download Form at www.The777Plan.com)

implementation. In order to do this, a good first step will be to plot (or group) the frequencies (how often we do things) together. In other words, for each task in each area of life, we have determined that we want to complete certain tasks on a daily, weekly, bi-weekly, quarterly, bi-annual or annual basis. We have also discovered that there are some desires that we want to complete either immediately or just once. Some tasks may need to be completed both immediately as well as frequently (e.g. daily, weekly, etc). Therefore, we should begin to plot (group) all of the frequencies of each task in each area of life together. We should plot the recurring things in the same group and we should plot the immediate things in the same group. This is important because it is with this information that we can begin to plan (schedule) what's done on an ongoing basis and what needs to be done immediately or just once.

Plotting: On-Going Action Steps

We should plot (group) all recurring (ongoing) similar action steps together. In order to do this, we should review each 777 Plan™ Worksheet for every area of life and then identify all action steps that are the same. In other words, we should plot (group) all Daily (D), Weekly or Bi-weekly (W/BW), Monthly (M), Quarterly (Q), Bi-annual (BA), and Annual (A) action steps together. Then, we should transfer that data onto The 777 Plan™ Plotting Form. Literally, we should list all of the Ds in the D column; list all of the Ws in the W column; list all the Ms in the M column etc. It's just that simple. *(See Diagrams 6.1 through 6.7 and Diagram 7 for an example of the process).*

Doing this will help us to easily identify what we do and when we do it on an ongoing basis. This is a critical step because our ongoing action steps will become routine and as a result we won't have to think about them as much. Eventually, we will be able to focus on digging out from the past by accomplishing those immediate or one-time tasks that have stacked up against us from the past.

Plot Immediate (or One-Time) Action Steps Together

Our immediate (I) or one-time action steps should be grouped together and ultimately should be used as our task list. First, we should go through every worksheet for every area of life and identify the tasks (action steps) that are immediate (I) or one time. Then, we should group (list) them all onto the (I) column (1st column) of The 777 Plan™ Plotting Form *(See Diagrams 6.1 through 6.7 and Diagram 7).*

Once we've done this, it is possible that the majority of our list will be comprised of critical priorities especially if things have stacked up against us over a course of time. But, steady the course. We should not try to do everything at once. We will need God's Knowledge, Wisdom and Spiritual Understanding in order to know what to do and when to do it.

Summary of The 777 Plan™ Plotting Process

STEP 1

Determine what your Main Areas of Desire are for every area of life. Then, list those areas on a 777 Plan™ Worksheet for every area. *(See Diagrams 6.1 through 6.7).*

Most people have seven main areas of desire and they are:

- ☐ Spiritual Desires
- ☐ Desires for House and Home
- ☐ Personal Care Desires
- ☐ Desires for Family and Friends
- ☐ Financial Desires
- ☐ Work/School Desires
- ☐ Desires for the Future
- ☐ ____________________
- ☐ ____________________
- ☐ ____________________

Note: you may have more than seven especially if you have a home business or other pursuit that you are pursuing simultaneously. In fact, you may need to do a separate 777 Plan™ for those other areas, if necessary.

STEP 2

Accomplish the following:

☐ Determine what overall tasks need to be accomplished in every area of life. Then, enter it onto each 777 Plan™ worksheet for every area of life. *(See first column of Diagrams 6.1 through 6.7).*

☐ Determine what action steps need to be taken in order to accomplish each overall task for every area of life. Then, enter them onto each 777 Plan™ worksheet for every area of life. *(See second Column of Diagrams 6.1 through 6.7).*

☐ Determine how often (the frequency) each action step should be taken in order to accomplish each overall task for every area of life. Then, enter them onto each 777 Plan™ worksheet for every area of life. *(See third Column of Diagrams 6.1 through 6.7).*

- **I** = Immediate or One-Time Action Steps
- **W** = Weekly Action Steps
- **M** = Monthly Action Steps
- **Q** = Quarterly Action Steps
- **A** = Annual Action Steps

☐ Determine what day or date (deadline) each action step will be taken in order to accomplish each overall task for every area of life. Then, enter them onto each 777 Plan™ worksheet for every area of life. *(See fourth and fifth Columns of Diagrams 6.1 through 6.7).*

☐ Determine how much time or money it may cost to accomplish each action step of each overall task for every area of life. Then, enter it onto each 777 Plan™ worksheet for every area of life. *(See sixth column of Diagrams 6.1 through 6.7).*

☐ Determine who is available to help you to accomplish each action step for each overall task for every area of life. Then, enter it onto each 777 Plan™ worksheet for every area of life. *(See Last Column of Diagrams 6.1 through 6.7).*

Diagram 6.1: Area of Life: Spiritual Desires

Tasks	Action Steps	Frequency	Complete Day/ Date		Cost	Helps/ Delegation
Deepen Relationship with God	Get up & Pray	D				
	Read the Word	D				
	Attend Bible Study	W	Wed		2 hr.	

Diagram 6.2: Area of Life: Desires for House & Home

Tasks	Action Steps	Frequency	Complete Day/ Date		Cost	Helps/ Delegation
Clean House	Vacuum	W	Sat		30min	
	Declutter/ File Paperwork	I/M	1st Sat			
Clean Clothes	Take Clothes to the Cleaner	I/W	Mon			

Diagram 6.3: Area of Life: Personal Care Desires

Tasks	Action Steps	Frequency	Complete Day/ Date		Cost	Helps/ Delegation
Grooming	Get Haircut	W	Sat am		30min	
Rest & Relaxation	Date Night with Spouse	W	Fri			
	Little Getaway with Spouse	Q		April Aug		

Diagram 6.4: Area of Life: Desires for Family & Friends

Tasks	Action Steps	Frequency	Complete Day/ Date		Cost	Helps/ Delegation
Stay in Touch	Call Mom	W	Wed			
	Call Dad	W	Fri am			
	Visit Grandmom	M	Sun			

Diagram 6.5: Area of Life: Financial Desires

Tasks	Action Steps	Frequency	Complete Day/ Date		Cost	Helps/ Delegation
Current Bills	Set up Autopay for Current Bills	I		Last Day/ Mo.		
	Set up Budget	I		Last Day/ Mo.		
	Review Finances	M				

Diagram 6.6: Area of Life: Work/School Desires

Tasks	Action Steps	Frequency	Complete Day/ Date		Cost	Helps/ Delegation
Gain & Maintain Order	Set up Filing System that Works for me	I				
	File Paperwork	W	Fri			
	Update & Review Computerized Schedule	D				

Diagram 7: 777 Plan™ Plotting Form

One-Time Immediate	Daily	Weekly/ Bi-Weekly	Monthly Bi-Monthly	Quarterly	Bi-Annual	Annual
Declutter/File Paperwork at Home	Get Up & Pray	Attend Bible Study (Wed)	Declutter/File Paperwork at Home	Take Little Getaway w/Spouse		
Take Clothes to Cleaners	Read the Word	Vacuum (Sat)	Review Finances			
Set up Autopay for All Current Bills	Update & Review Computerized Schedule	Take Clothes to Cleaner (Mon)	Visit Grandmom			
Set up Budget	Complete Manuscript	Get Haircut (Sat)				
Set up Filing System that Works for Me		Date Night with Spouse (Fri)				
Complete Manuscript		Call Mom (Mon)				
		Call Dad (Fri am)				
		File Paperwork at Work (Fri pm)				
		Update Blog (Mon pm)				

Planning (Scheduling): A Word on Time

I have only just a minute, only 60 seconds in it,
forced upon me, can't refuse it.
Didn't seek it, didn't choose it, but it's up to me to use it.
I must suffer if I lose it, Give account if I abuse it.
Just a tiny little minute– but eternity is in it.

Dr. Benjamin Elijah Mays
President Emeritus, Morehouse College

Now we are equipped to start planning (scheduling) when we are going to accomplish our ongoing and immediate action steps. We've already grouped like kind action steps together on the 777 Plan™ Plotting Form *(Diagram 7)*. Therefore, our next step is to transfer those data onto our manual or automated calendars.

This is where the rubber hits the road and where theory grows closer to practice. I say grows closer because transferring information from one sheet of paper to another doesn't mean we are going to actually do what we've transferred. However, I have discovered that once I've put information into a calendar, it becomes crystallized in my mind and it becomes more likely that I will take action upon it. But, if I don't record it then, most likely, I won't get around to it, or I will do it at the last minute. That is always stressful.

This process requires maintenance and endurance. Former U.S. Supreme Court Justice, Sandra Day O'Conner once said, "Slaying the dragon of delay is no sport for the short winded." Therefore, catch your breath and let's keep it moving. Come on, let's take another step. Let's start planning how and when we are going to dig out from the past, manage the present, and enter into the future.

Plan (Schedule) Ongoing Action Steps

The 777 Plan™ Plotting Form enables us to determine how frequently we do what we do. As you know, the frequencies are grouped on a Daily (D), Weekly (W), Bi-Weekly (BW), Monthly (M), Bi-Monthly (BM), Quarterly (Q), Bi-Annual (BA), and Annual (A) basis. We can now begin to schedule the groups of actions accordingly. For example, on Diagram 7, you may notice that I get up and pray, read The Word (or at least I desire to), on a daily basis. Also, when I was writing this book, I vowed to get up early and write and revise for an hour or two until the manuscript was finished. Thank God I did or else I would have continued to procrastinate on writing this book on overcoming procrastination. I digress. Also, when I get to work, I review my computerized schedule and task list daily so that I can ensure that my schedule is up to date. The point here is that all of that information is readily available and grouped together on The

777 Plan™ Plotting Form and is scheduled on my calendar so that I do not have to "think" about it. Instead, I can just do what needs to be done.

The process is the same for the weekly, monthly, quarterly, and annual action steps I take as well. For the actions I take weekly and monthly, I have also determined the days and dates that I would like to accomplish certain actions. Therefore, all I have to do is find those days and dates and write them into my calendar. Since they are ongoing, all I need to do is record them on the days and dates on which they recur and they are there until I am ready to make a change. This works really well if you use a personal digital assistant (a PDA) or some other type of computerized calendar because it reminds us when it is time to perform an action step.

If you use a manual calendar, then you will have to re-write the information at least every month to make sure your schedule is planned out for that month. I have graduated from using a manual (paper) calendar because I like the idea of not having to re-write my recurring action items every time I review my 777 Plan™ which is every month.

Plan (Schedule) Immediate or One Time Action Steps

After I schedule my ongoing actions steps, I then review the immediate and one-time column of the 777 Plan™ Plotting Form (it's the first column) *(See Diagram 7)*. I prioritize what's critical (A Priority); what's important but not critical (B Priority); and what's not that important but should be done at some point (C Priority). I transfer the A's, B's and C's onto a main task list in my hand held computer and I review it daily and weekly to monitor what has been done and what needs to be done. The ongoing items are scheduled first, then the immediate actions are accomplished based on priority. That way, both immediate (past and current) and recurring items get accomplished simultaneously. At some point, the task list of past due desires and obligations dwindles. Then, it becomes a list of future pursuits.

Now, with all of this said, you will discover that there are probably several one-time or immediate action steps that are all either critically past due or are equally as important. The tendency will be to start doing ALL of the things that you have not done. I would suggest not doing this because you will have too much to do. Instead, I would suggest looking closely at what's most important and critical. Then, begin to whittle those critical tasks off the list first. Dale Carnegie said, "Do the hard jobs first. The easy jobs will take care of themselves."

At the same time, when you start confronting the backlog of past due and unfulfilled desires and obligations, other actions steps will be added to your task list. This is the case because past due items usually have hidden hoops that have to be jumped through before they can be closed out. However, you will not know what those hoops are until you take the initial action step. This must be planned for. For example, I remember I once procrastinated and let my driver's license expire. Of course, that can happen to anyone right? I digress. At any rate, because I did not take care of it in enough time, I had to take the driver's test all over again. That was a hoop that I had not planned for when I finally decided to go down and get my driver's license renewed. These hoops await those of us who let things back up and stack up.

Nevertheless, do not be discouraged if your list of immediate items grows instead of shrinks. You will reach a point when the additional steps will be completely eradicated. As a result, the backlog from the past will be eradicated once and for all. Trust me when I tell you, this is probably the most difficult part of the process. But, it is worth it to keep chipping away at it because if we give up too soon, the backlog will never go away and the stress that comes along with the backlog will never go away, and we will not be able to reach the land of no lack. That is horrible.

When there is a hill to climb,
don't think that waiting will make it smaller.

Anonymous

Automated Planners and Calendars

In this age of technology, increasingly, many people use automated calendars, planners and smartphones. The biggest advantage in using an automated planner or calendar is, once we've entered ongoing items and immediate tasks, those items do not have to be re-entered into the system. Instead, they pop up as reminders on our PDAs and computer terminals. Our only caution is, if something happens to our PDA or computer system then we may lose our elaborate plan. However, if we've gone all the way through the 777 Plan™ process, then we should have saved a hard copy of the 777 Plan™ Plotting Form. Therefore, the only thing we will need to do is re-enter the information into a new automated calendar.

Plan (Schedule) The Day to Review The 777 Plan™

I review my 777 Plan™ overall at least once a month (*e.g.* usually the first Saturday of every month). I actually schedule that action step as a monthly, recurring event in my computerized calendar. Even though it is difficult, I try to keep that appointment because I am able to assess and reassess what's working in my life and what's not. Also, on that day I am also able to schedule new action steps. Therefore, we must be determined to follow through and follow up with our strategy because it helps us to break the back of slack and it keeps us on track.

7 Months to Achieve

Joshua addressed the People of Israel and asked:

"How long are you going to sit around on your hands, putting off taking possession of the land that GOD, the God of your ancestors, has given you? Pick three men from each tribe so I can commission them. They will survey and map the land, showing the inheritance due each tribe, and report back to me. They will divide it into seven parts. Judah will stay in its territory in the south and the people of Joseph will keep to their place in the north."

Joshua 18:3-5 (The Message Bible)

After Joshua asked the Israelites how long they were going to be slack in taking possession of the land that was already conquered for them, he immediately began to develop a strategy to get them going. He commissioned three men from each of the slack tribes to go and describe (give an account of) and divide (break down into achievable parts) the land. Also, he instructed them to bring the description and division back to him. Josephus, an ancient Jewish historian, suggested that it took the 21 men about 7 months to achieve that task. Thus, we can glean some practical wisdom and apply it to the implementation of The 777 Plan.™

It should take about 7 months to break old habits and establish new ones. Simultaneously, it should take the same amount of time to begin to see our paradigms shift from living presently in the past to living peacefully and progressively in the future. The process should continue as a way of life even after the 7 month period.

In fact, I am usually very productive when I follow the process. But, when I do not, I am not very productive and I become more and more stressed. The beautiful thing is, if I miss a meeting with myself or if I fall away from the process, I forgive myself; pick myself up; and brush myself off. Then, I pick up where I left off. You should do the same thing!

We can review, restart or re-do the process whenever we need to. It is our plan and therefore we can work it anyway and anytime we want to. Isn't that a blessing? It sure is. So, let's work it so that we can break the back of slack and enter into the land of no lack.

Words of Encouragement

We sometimes say the cliché: God is an on time God. Well, since that is true, then we too should be on time in doing what needs to be done. However, this is very difficult if we do not plan our schedules with the intent of keeping them as closely as possible. Also, it is also very difficult if we are overwhelmed with a mountain unfulfilled past due obligations and mismanaged current desires that eventually morph into past due obligations. The question becomes, how can we possibly get anything done under these circumstances? Well, the unfortunate reality is, we can't.

Our issue of time management becomes even more important when unforeseen things occur. When something unforeseen happens, then our lives are often thrust into a whirlwind. Whatever we thought we were going to get done gets trampled by the urgency of the critical situation that we are now forced to face. However, if we have plotted and planned our course, we will have a road map to navigate our way back on track to the land of no lack.

Yes, plotting and planning takes some time and energy. However, let me ask you, how much time and energy do you spend thinking about, but not doing anything about, all you desire to do? I would imagine your answer will probably be: "too much." What a drain that is on the membrane. Just think, that same amount of energy could be spent reaching your goals and doing the things you want to do. Therefore, be encouraged because the victor gets the spoils. Immediately you will begin to see the results that come from getting a snapshot of everything you've got going on. This is the case even though your list might be exhaustive. That is a good thing even if it looks chaotic.

Remember, God knows how to transform chaos into order and He knows how to instruct us on how to overcome procrastination, break the back of slack, and finally enter into the land of no lack. Thus, it is worth it to go all the way through the process. Also, when you take these steps, you may experience a wide range of emotions. On one end of the spectrum, you may get exhausted and discouraged just looking at, perhaps for the first time, all you've got going on and all that needs to be done in your life.

On the other end of the spectrum, your mind will become relieved because finally, all you've been thinking about, will be emptied out of your mind, plotted onto a sheet of paper, and planned in a calendar. That is a much better way to strategically deal with what needs to be dealt with.

Prayer:

Father, it seems like I have so much to do but I have so little time to do everything that I desire. Some things have stacked up against me from the past, and there are some current things that I can't manage. There are also some things that I desire to accomplish in the future but I can't pursue them because I have so much going on.

I acknowledge that I need a strategic plan to help me to gain, re-gain and maintain order. Father, please help me to implement the plan and please give me knowledge, wisdom and spiritual understanding, so that I may accomplish my desires.

In The Name of The Lord Jesus Christ, I pray, Amen!

Summary of Scriptures:

Joshua 18:3-6 (The Message Bible)

Matthew 6:3

†

Chapter Eight
Desire and Diligence

The sluggard craves and gets nothing, but the desires of the diligent are fully satisfied.

Proverb 13:4 (NIV)

Desire dwells and diligence propels. However, desire remains just desire without taking diligent steps to accomplish it. Many procrastinators desire to do things, but we seldom accomplish what we desire. That is frustrating. However, when diligently we take action, our desires become accomplishments. In other words, our desires are what we long to achieve but diligence, which is painstaking steady effort, enables us to accomplish what we desire.

In addition, when our diligent efforts are coupled with a doable plan, accomplishment will be the end result. For example, The 777 Plan™ is a plan to gain, regain, or maintain order, break the back of slack, and enter into the land of no lack. But, if we do not diligently work the plan, then, most likely, our desires will not get accomplished. Now, that's torment—to have a plan to fulfill our desires but never achieve it. *"The desire of the slothful killeth him; for his hands refuse to labour."* (Proverb 21:25)

Indecision, fear, worry and shame cause our desires to go unfulfilled and they cause hardship in our lives. For instance, *"He becometh poor that dealeth with a slack hand: but the hand of the diligent maketh rich"* (Proverb 10:4). *"The hand of the diligent shall bear rule: but the slothful shall be under tribute."* (Proverb 12:24) *"The soul of the sluggard desireth, and hath nothing: but the soul of the diligent shall be made fat."* (Proverb 13:4)

On the other hand, diligence makes us rich, causes us to bear rule, and enables our souls to be made fat. In other words, diligence turns our desires into accomplishments and enables us to live in the land of no lack. However, diligence is not cheap. Instead, we have to pay a premium that requires us to be relentless, undeterred, and undistracted in our pursuit to accomplish what we desire. In order to illustrate that type of diligence, let's consider the ant—you know that insect that relentlessly crawls while carrying twice her weight in order to fulfill her desires. She does this even when faced with the danger of being stepped on. Ants amaze me because even if stepped on, they keep crawling. They will not stop even if they have one leg left with which to crawl. Now that's diligence! We can learn from them.

Consider The Ant

Go to the ant, thou sluggard; consider her ways, and be wise: which having no guide, overseer, or ruler, provideth her meat in the summer, and gathereth her food in the harvest.

Proverbs 6:6-8

In Proverbs 6:6-8, King Solomon provides us with some practical instruction on becoming diligent. The ant in the passage is diligent. She takes the painstaking, steady effort to accomplish her desires. In order to be diligent, she does a couple of things: she knows what to do; and she does what she knows. Therefore, we should do likewise.

- **Know What to Do**
- **Do What You Know**

Know What To Do

Go to the ant, thou sluggard; consider her ways, and be wise: which having no guide, overseer, or ruler...

Proverbs 6:6-7

The ant is diligent because she knows what to do. She does not have anyone standing over top of her telling her what to do. Instead, she just does it and keeps on doing it until her desires have been accomplished. Perhaps she has a gnosis *(a knowing from God)* of what must be done and how to do it. Can it be possible that she too can hear the voice of wisdom and understanding crying from the inside out? I believe so. Since God created her too, I imagine that He communicates with her in a way that she can understand Him. He must be the one who guides and drives her to be so diligent in accomplishing her desires. Otherwise, why else would He use her as an example of diligence for us to consider?

She provides in the summer and gathers in the harvest. In essence, she knows when to gather and when to provide what has been gathered. The ant is aware of the times and seasons, therefore, her life is in order and she lives without lack. She goes forth with diligence seemingly without effort because she knows what to do.

If the ant can know and be diligent, then we can know more and be more diligent in accomplishing our desires. With God's knowledge, wisdom and understanding guiding us from the inside out, and with the implementation of The 777 Plan,™ there is absolutely nothing we cannot accomplish. Every desire, in every area of life, can be accomplished and we can live without lack. In fact, knowing what to do should inspire us to be diligent in doing what needs to be done. It's just when we don't know, we end up slack, slothful or sluggish. Therefore, the first thing we should do is step back from self and then step up to God so that we can know what to do. He will unveil knowledge of His will, His wisdom, and He will give us spiritual understanding so that we can go forth with diligence to accomplish our desires. The inner drive to accomplish Gods' will (no lack) comes from God. He lights us up on the inside with His Holy Spirit and inspires us to go forth. However, we determine to what extent the fire will burn, by diligently seeking Him. And, it is up to us to be diligent in doing what He is guiding us to do.

Do What You Know

...which having no guide, overseer, or ruler,
provideth her meat in the summer,
and gathereth her food in the harvest.

Proverbs 6:7-8

Not only does the ant diligently provide and gather, because she knows what to do, she takes action and works her plan. She does what she knows and will not stop until she gets there and has returned home with her desired prize (*accomplished her desires).* As we go forth to do what we know, even if we are not totally sure what we know, one thing we do know is that God desires that we would live lives that lack nothing. That means that we can turn our desires, in every area of life, into accomplishments with diligence. Also with diligence, we can dig out from the past, manage the present and enter into the future by implementing the 777 Plan.™

Simply put, we should do what we know and ultimately we will overcome procrastination God's way, break the back of slack, and never go back with our diligence. As we are working our plan, there are few additional things we can do to be effectively diligent.

They are the following:

- **Be Realistic**
- **Fight One Battle At a Time**
- **Be Thorough**
- **Beware of Bad Desires**

Be Realistic

Diligence requires us to be realistic about what we attempt to undertake because digging out from the past, managing the present and accomplishing future desires requires a lot of time and energy. Also, many of us are starting by staring at a mountain of past due and perhaps critically important unfulfilled desires and obligations. They may appear to be insurmountable and overwhelming. At the same time, we have to manage our current obligations that just keep rolling in from every side. As a result, we may be forced to put our future desires on hold because we are so bogged down with past and present desires

With all of this in mind, we have to be realistic about what we can accomplish and when we can accomplish it. This is not to say that we cannot accomplish some things quickly. However, everything that we want to accomplish cannot be accomplished at once. If so, there will be way too much to do. We have to be realistic about our undertakings if we are going to remain diligent.

This also underscores the importance of going all the way through the 777 Plan™ process because it will help us to sort out what we can readily attack and what we can't. Also, we should be realistic because, along the way, we will experience some setbacks and exhaustion and the old slack, slothful and sluggish self will still try to bear rule in our lives. At the same time, being realistic will help make the journey sustainable. You can do it!

Fight One Battle At a Time

The seven procrastinating tribes were so close but yet so far in entering into the land of no lack. As soon as they had crossed the River Jordan, they were forced to fight the battle of Jericho—the biggest and hardest battle of them all. After they fought that battle, then they had to fight 30 additional battles over the course of a number of years before they got to Shiloh. Most importantly, they had to fight one battle at a time. Otherwise, they would have been too overwhelmed and would have been defeated.

Our experience will be no different. As we diligently commence our journey to overcome procrastination God's way, we too will have our own personal Jericho's to fight. At the same time, we will have to fight other battles before we can officially proclaim that we have broken the back of slack and entered into the land of no lack. Therefore, if we follow the example of the seven procrastinating tribes, then we should first conquer the Jericho (biggest battle) that continues to cause us to procrastinate in going forward in our lives. Remember Dale Carnegie's quote, "Do the hard jobs first. The easy jobs will take care of themselves."

For example, after I developed and then began to test the 777 Plan™ I discovered that there was so much to do. At first, I tried to do everything simultaneously. However, I soon discovered that was unrealistic. I felt like a computer that had too many applications open at the same time. I felt like I was going to crash. I had to step back and review my overall situation and then I decided to do what was most critical. I chose Jericho, the Battle Royale: gaining order in my home. I chose that first because everything else hinged on me having order. I had to find a place for everything, develop a system of organization, and declutterize my home.

Before I got married, I had a lot of paperwork and clutter to sift through and as a result I couldn't think, pray or be diligent at doing anything. Therefore, I had to start with that project first. I am not so sure how realistic I was because I did it the hard way. I did it by myself. But, since that was my Jericho, I had to fight it relentlessly and diligently. By doing so, I built up stamina and gained confidence. Ultimately, I became even more diligent in gaining order in every other area of my life and I was able to conquer the remaining smaller battles. In essence, I fought one battle at a time and the smaller battles became much easier to fight because I had already conquered Jericho. Many desires have been accomplished since then but I am still working it out. Nevertheless, the struggle is much easier now than it ever has been. You should conquer your Jericho first. You can do it!

Ask yourself these questions:

Food For Thought

- **What is your biggest battle?**
- **What's causing you to procrastinate ?**
- **Is it a lack of vision?**
- **Do you have lack of knowledge of God's will, God's wisdom, or Spiritual understanding when making God decisions?**
- **Do the lions of fear, worry or shame roar against you?**
- **Is it difficult to confront what needs to be confronted?**
- **Do you have a lack of order overall, or in any area of desire in your life?**
- **Is it difficult for you to get started because you are so bogged down? What is it?**

Whatever it is, attack the biggest, baddest battle first and the smaller battles get easier to conquer.

Do the hard jobs first.
The easy jobs will take care of themselves.

Dale Carnegie

Be Thorough

As the Lord commanded Moses his servant,
so did Moses command Joshua, and so did Joshua;
he left nothing undone of all that the Lord
commanded Moses.

Joshua 11:15

In order to be diligent, we must take the painstaking but steady effort to complete every action step of every overall task in every area of life. It is an arduous and ongoing undertaking but it is not impossible. The 777 Plan™ will help us to identify and then prioritize which immediate and ongoing tasks and steps need to be taken. With both, nothing should be left undone.

This type of thoroughness is rare because most people are not willing or able to take the steady painstaking effort to diligently work at a thing until every action step has been taken. The reasons for that vary, but at a minimum, misperception (negative thinking), the underlying root causes of procrastination (fear, worry and shame), sheer exhaustion as well as a lack of order are the culprits. As a result, we end up frustrated and lacking because we have not completed each action step for every overall task in every area of life. For example, Proverb 12:27 says, *"The slothful man roasteh not that which he took in hunting; but the substance of a diligent is precious."* In other words, the slothful man got up (probably early in the morning) and put on his hunting clothes, lugged his bow and arrows through the bush and trees. Then, he probably tracked, trapped, killed and carried away his prey (and his gear) all the way back home. But, because the man did not roast what he caught, it probably spoiled and he probably went another day hungry. Therefore, the man was still slothful because he did not complete the process. It must have been frustrating for him to go through all of that and still not fully accomplish his desires, or even worse, still live in lack.

Unfortunately, this scenario is common amongst procrastinators. We start stuff but we don't finish it. For us, starting a project is easy because it does not take much time or energy. However, completing a project is not as easy because we either realize that it is going to take more time or energy than we thought at first, or we get distracted by something else. This is the turning back point. We say to ourselves, "That's too much," or "That's going to take too long" or even, "I'll get back to that later." But, for many of us, we don't get back to it. Or, if we do, because so much time has elapsed, we have to start all over again.

As a result, we end up frustrated and lacking like the slothful man because we have put forth some effort, received a false sense of accomplishment, but walked away with no real results because we did not complete the project. This is the case even if we complete a substantial portion of a project. A project is still just a project until it has been completely accomplished. William James said, "Nothing is so fatiguing as the eternal hanging on of an uncompleted task." Therefore, we must be diligent in chipping away at completing every step of every task, until the area of desire has been fulfilled.

On the other hand, when we complete everything, we experience great satisfaction in our souls. Proverb 13:19 says, *"Desire accomplished is sweet to the soul."* It is possible and probable when we leave nothing undone. However, we should take caution because bad desires defeat our ability to diligently accomplish our desires.

Beware of Bad Desires

...There is an accursed thing in the midst of thee O Israel:
thou canst not stand before thine enemies,
until ye take away the accursed thing from among you.

Joshua 7:13

Bad desires are lusts or cravings that come from the flesh. They can be addictions, wrong motives, bad attitudes, negative perspectives, or even sin. Also, bad desires thwart our ability to be diligent. In the Old Testament, bad desires were called "accursed things." For the Israelites, right after they fought and won at Jericho, they came up against an enemy made up of thirty-six people. However, since one of the Israelites had taken for himself some silver and gold that belonged to the defeated Canaanites, the entire Israelite Army of three thousand men got defeated. The accursed things were his greed and pride that polluted the spiritual atmosphere and caused them to be defeated.

So it is with us. If we have bad desires, our results may be similar to those of the Israelites. We may be troubled (Joshua 6:18). Our hearts may melt and become as water (be given to fear) (Joshua 7:5). We may find ourselves out of the presence of God (Joshua 7:12). Or, we may find ourselves defeated (Joshua 7:12). All of those things form a wedge between our God-inspired desires and our diligent pursuit to turn our desires into God-ordained accomplishments. In essence, bad desires cause us to pause (procrastinate) in breaking the back of slack and entering into the land of no lack. However, when we conquer those bad desires, and replace them with God-inspired desires, they will become accomplishments, and our souls will be satisfied.

A Word on Social Media Addictions & Other Time Wasters

He that is slothful in his work
is brother to him that is a great waster.

Proverb 18:9

In this electronic age, many people spend a lot of time on social media, surfing the net, email and other electronic mediums. I make special mention of this particular issue here because the culprit that looms underneath and causes us to squander our time is a bad desire. Recently, I conducted an impromptu and informal survey on the social media site that I belong to. Most people who responded admitted spending an average of one to two hours a day on the site. That is a lot of time if we multiply two hours a day times thirty days per month. That means sixty hours a month are spent on social media. Most people work forty hours a week.

I would venture to say that most people actually spend more time than what was admitted to in the survey. Imagine if all that time was spent digging out from the past, managing the present, or accomplishing future pursuits? We would be able to break the back of slack and enter into the land of no lack. Therefore, I must ask, is social media an accursed thing? No, I don't believe it is because I have made some very meaningful connections and re-connections through social media. However, the thing that looms underneath and entices us to squander so much time might be. Either way, we should monitor how much time we spend on social media because wasting time hinders our progress in reaching the land of no lack.

What's Really Going On Here?

Social media has a pull to it that is much like an addiction. Ultimately, that pull causes us to be slack, slothful or sluggish. Therefore, if we want to overcome procrastination God's way, we should be aware of anything that looms underneath and distracts, enchants or entices us to squander so much of our time. Again, this is not a crusade against the use of technology because it is here to stay. Instead, it is my intent to expose the bad desires (distractions, addictions, lusts and cravings, bad motives, negative perspectives) that loom underneath and kill our desire to pursue diligently the no lack life that God has promised us. In Beth Moore's book, *Get Out of That Pit,* she says, "Satan's definitive goal is to reap destruction, but that is rarely his starting point. His usual opening is distraction." She further suggests that he employs "a well-contrived program based on a step-by-step progressive plan..." She submits that "a distraction becomes an addiction and then it leads to destruction (Distraction + Addiction = Destruction)."

In this case, the distraction is the allure that social media brings and the addiction is the satisfaction we feel when someone reacts favorably to something we have to say or the connection or re-connection we have made with friends. As a result, we keep going back for more and we spend more time than we should. Ultimately, the no lack life that God has promised gets destroyed. A distraction is a distraction no matter what medium is being used (*e.g.*, social media, internet, texting, emailing, cable television, or anything else that causes us to squander our time).

Conquer Your Bad Desires

Up, sanctify the people, and say,
Sanctify yourselves against tomorrow:
for thus saith the LORD God of Israel, there is an accursed thing in the midst of thee, O Israel:
thou canst not stand before thine enemies,
until ye take away the accursed thing from among you.

Joshua 7:13

God gave Joshua a Word concerning conquering bad desires. He said, *"Up, sanctify the people, and say, Sanctify yourselves against tomorrow: for thus saith the LORD God of Israel, there is an accursed thing in the midst of thee, O Israel: thou canst not stand before thine enemies, until ye take away the accursed thing from among you."* (Joshua 7:13). In the Hebrew, sanctify means to pronounce something as clean. In the Greek, it means to separate. Thus, God was instructing the Israelites, and us, to separate our selves from our fleshly desires, and then pronounce our desires to be clean. That requires confession and repentance as well as discipline. 1 John 1:8-9 says, *"If we say that we have no sin, we deceive ourselves, and the truth is not in us. If we confess our sins, He is faithful and just to forgive us our sins, and to cleanse us from all unrighteousness."* God wants to cleanse us and replace our bad desires with His desires so that, with our diligence, those desires will be accomplished and no lack will be achieved in our lives.

If we acknowledge that we have some impure desires, then God will cleanse us with The Blood of The Lord Jesus Christ and our bad desires will be conquered. He will cleanse the spiritual atmosphere and impart His desire into our souls. Then, we will begin to thrive in the Kingdom of God where *"all these things will be added unto us"* and we will be able to completely declare that we have overcome the underlying things that loom underneath and cause us to procrastinate. However, we must have the desire to have God-inspired desires. When we do, *"He will fulfill the desire of them that fear Him: He also will hear their cry, and will save them."*(Psalm 145:19).

- **What are your desires? Do you desire to have God-inspired desires? Are you willing to be diligent in turning your God-inspired desires into God-ordained accomplishments?**

- **Or, do you have any bad desires such as: addictions, wrong motives, bad attitudes, or negative perspectives? If so, are you willing to sanctify those bad desires and replace them with God-inspired desires?**

God will fulfill our desires and will help us to break the back of slack so that we can enter into the land of no lack. Not only is it possible, it is a promise. In addition, diligence fueled by the knowledge of God's will, Wisdom and Spiritual understanding, empowers us to achieve whatever God wants to achieve through us in this lifetime.

Prayer:

Father, create in me a clean heart, and renew a right spirit within me. Father, also, please create in me a desire to accomplish what You desire for my life and a desire to be diligent in accomplishing what You desire.

Father, please give me Your knowledge, wisdom and spiritual understanding so that I can know what to do and do what I know.

I also need help to overcome the bad desires, addictions, negative perspectives, or sin that has caused me to procrastinate in my life. In Jesus' Name, I pray, Amen!

Summary of Scriptures:

Proverb 13:4 (NIV)

Proverb 21:25

Proverb 10:4

Proverb 12:24

Joshua 11:15

Proverb 12:27

Proverb 13:19

Joshua 7:13

Joshua 6:18

Joshua 7:5

Joshua 7:12

Proverb 18:9

1 John 1:8-9

Psalm 145:19

Notes

†

Chapter Nine
Vitality and Virtue

For the enemy hath persecuted my soul; he hath smitten my life down to the ground; he hath made me to dwell in darkness, as those that have been long dead. Therefore, is my spirit overwhelmed within me...

Psalm 143:3-4

The truth of the matter is, most of us desire to overcome procrastination, break the back of slack, and enter into the land of no lack, but we can't because we are exhausted or overwhelmed.

Simply put, we procrastinate (put things off until a later time) because we are just too worn out. We have tried and tried to get going but to no avail, nothing has worked. We are still slack, slothful or sluggish and to some degree many have given in or given up. We have acquiesced because we just don't have the strength or energy to do anything differently.

That is probably what the seven procrastinating tribes went through. They were probably utterly exhausted and overwhelmed and as a result were slack to take possession of the land of no lack.

Remember, they had to cross the River Jordan and then fight the Battle of Jericho. I'm sure both events took a lot of energy. Then, they had to fight 30 more battles over the course of a number of years. They went from one stressful, time consuming, and de-energizing event to another. They must have been worn out, shell shocked, traumatized, or whatever. So when they finally arrived at Shiloh they probably just wanted to rest. That's probably why they stayed there so long. They probably needed some supernatural energy to break the back of slack and enter the land of no lack. To get them going, Joshua appealed to their souls by asking them how long they were going to allow themselves to be slack and live a life of lack.

Therefore, let me appeal to your soul. How long are you going to be slack, slothful or sluggish in taking possession of the life of no lack that God has ordained for you? Perhaps, someone may answer with a sigh and say, "Just for a little while longer; just let me catch my breath." Well, if that is what you really mean then, ok. But, if you are too overwhelmed or exhausted and you don't know exactly how to regain your strength, then that is a different situation.

If you are completely maxed out and just don't know what to do, then let me make a couple of suggestions. However, before I do, let me define my terms. The soul (the inner man) is the place where our hearts and minds work cohesively to store, link and interact with God's presence. In Ephesians 3:16, Paul prayed that the church at Ephesus would *"be strengthened with might by His Spirit in the inner man."* In essence, the soul is the reservoir where The Holy Spirit lives. At the moment we establish a relationship with God through The Lord Jesus Christ, God satiates (fills to the full) and strengthens our souls with His presence (The Holy Spirit). Jeremiah 31:25 says, *"For I have satiated the weary soul, and I have replenished every sorrowful soul."*

It is with this satiation that we are empowered, replenished, and strengthened with God's supernatural (dunamis) power especially when our souls have been smitten (attacked and afflicted) down to the ground. Therefore, if your soul is weary and depleted from all that you have endured, then please be encouraged because you have a reservoir of God's supernatural power stored inside of you. It is from this reservoir that you will be revived and restored back to a level of energy that can get you up and going once again.

This is how God does it. He quickens us with vitality and with His virtue. To quicken means God brings us back to life again. He makes us profoundly aware of His presence and power that dwells in the inner man. He then creates a surge of power in us that so obviously does not belong to us. It flows like a steady stream or like a bolt of lightning. Either way, it is available. He brings us back to life especially when we are at our weakest point. In Romans 8:11, Paul reminds us that, *"If the Spirit of Him that raised up Jesus from the dead dwell in you, He that raised up Christ from the dead shall also quicken your mortal bodies by His Spirit that dwelleth in you."*

The steady stream flow of power is God's vitality. It permeates our minds, bodies and souls. Acts 17:28 says, *"for in Him we live, move, and have our being."* According to Isaiah 40:29, *"He giveth power to the faint; and to them that have no might, He increaseth strength."*

The flow that quickens like a bolt of lightning is God's virtue. Virtue is a specific dosage of God's power for a specific challenge. God's virtue has the potency and efficacy to overcome every issue known to humankind including the things that loom underneath in our souls and cause us to procrastinate. For example, God supernaturally quickened several people with His virtue when their souls were beat down. For instance, in Luke 6:17-19, a great multitude of people had gathered to hear the Lord Jesus Christ speak and to be healed of their diseases. They were vexed with a number of spirits which hindered them from making progress in their lives. The whole multitude of people sought to touch Jesus and when they did, virtue went out of Him and He healed them all. In another instance, in Luke 8:43-48, there was a woman who had an issue of blood (internal bleeding) for twelve (12) years. She was financially broke, and physically and mentally tired of her condition. But as soon as she touched the border of Jesus' garment, immediately, her issue was resolved by the transfer of God's virtue.

In order for us to be quickened (empowered and brought back to life) with God's vitality and virtue, we should do what others have done. We should do at least three things:

- **Get Empowered**
- **Take a Sabbath**
- **Take Action**

Get Empowered: Reach & Ask for the Power of God

In order to get empowered, we should ask God through prayer to release His dunamis power which is located in the reservoir of our souls. For example, in Psalm 143:6, when King David's soul was under attack and when he felt beat down to the ground, he stretched forth his hands as he thirsted for God's presence in his soul. He asked God to quicken him and destroy the things that afflicted his soul (Psalm 143:11-12). In similar examples, in Luke 6:17-19, those who were vexed by unclean spirits, and the woman in Luke 8:43-48, who had the issue of blood, did the same thing. They all reached forth to Jesus. The multitude and the woman touched Him and the virtue went out of Him. He empowered, and then healed them all.

God is no respecter of persons. He will do the same for us if we reach for Him and ask Him for a surge or a steady stream of His dunamis power. God wants to empower us so that we may continue our journey to the land of no lack. We should take a minute and step back from ourselves (our flesh) or from whatever is holding us back. Then, we should step up to The Lord Jesus Christ, by faith, and reach forth with the expectancy that He will bring us back to life again like He did with King David, the multitudes, and the woman with the issue of blood. He will release His vitality and His virtue. Thus, we will be able to dig out from the past, manage the present, enter into the future, overcome procrastination God's way, break the back of slack, slothfulness and sluggishness, and then take possession of the land of no lack that God has promised to us.

Take a Sabbath

For in six days the LORD made the heavens
and the earth, the sea, and all that is in them,
but He rested on the seventh day.
Therefore the LORD blessed the Sabbath day
and made it holy.

Exodus 20:11 (NIV)

Being supernaturally empowered does not mean that we become super human, and it certainly does not mean that we should continue to run ourselves into the ground. Instead, it means that we are empowered to accomplish all of the things that God ordains for our lives. That includes breaking the back of slack and entering into the land of no lack. It also means that we acquire Knowledge of God's Will, God's Wisdom and Spiritual Understanding. With such, we will know when to hold 'em and when to fold 'em.

For example, God used wisdom and power to create the earth in six days. Then, He sanctified the seventh day for Sabbath. In the Hebrew, Sabbath literally means intermission. In other words, God created for six days and took an intermission (rested) on the seventh day. Certainly, God could have done everything in one moment but I surmise that He walked us all the way through the process to provide us with an example of how we ought to live our lives. In fact, in Exodus 23:12, God strongly encouraged the Children of Israel to follow His example. He said, *"Six days thou shalt do thy work, and on the seventh day thou shalt rest..."* We should do the same. We should use the knowledge, wisdom and spiritual understanding that God has given us and apply it to our lives. That is what it is there for.

Now, of course God blessed the seventh day for worship. But after worship, there is nothing like a Sunday afternoon rest (or Saturday if that's the day you worship). It rejuvenates the body so that we can be ready to work on the first work day of the week. The human body can only take but so much. Also, there is something to be said about taking vacations. Sometimes we need a prolonged intermission so that we can recharge our batteries and get it going once again. It does not have to be a long vacation. It can be a few days somewhere close by. Either way, we should purpose to have down time.

My wife and I purpose to rest on Sunday afternoons after worship, and we take mini-vacations every three or four months or so. We also plan an extended vacation, for at least a week, once a year. In fact, I include those desires in my 777 Plan.™ If you can swing it, then I highly recommend it. If you can't, then I encourage you to take whatever time you can for an intermission. It is critical in maintaining your vitality and your virtue. Also, it is important to note that there is a difference between taking an intermission and loving sleep.

Taking an intermission is a temporary pause in our painstaking effort to break the back of slack and ultimately enter into the land of no lack. However, loving sleep is when we have fallen and won't get up or when we have chosen to stay in our uncomfortable comfort zones, like the Children of Israel who stayed at Shiloh for far too long. We should take caution because poverty is the end result of both situations. Proverbs 20:13 says, *"Love not sleep, lest thou come to poverty."* Proverbs 6:9-11 (NKJV) asks, *"How long will you slumber, O sluggard? When will you rise from your sleep? A little sleep, a little slumber, a little folding of the hands to sleep—so shall your poverty come on you like a prowler, and your need like an armed man."* With this in mind, we should take regular intermissions but we should not love to sleep. Instead, we should take action and continue to take action so that we can overcome procrastination God's way and so that we can live the no lack lives God has ordained.

Take Action Now

"Don't wait. The time will never be just right."

Napoleon Hill

"How soon not now, becomes never."

Dr. Martin Luther King, Jr.

"Now is the accepted time, not tomorrow,
not some more convenient season. It is today that our best
work can be done and not some future day or future year.
It is today that we fit ourselves
for the greater usefulness of tomorrow.
Today is the seed time, now are the hours of work, and
tomorrow comes the harvest and the playtime."

W. E. B. DuBois

There is no better time than the present to utilize the virtue and vitality that God has poured into our souls and begin to accomplish our desires. We will be able to walk in God's vision, make Godly decisions with knowledge, wisdom and spiritual understanding, confront what needs to be confronted, and gain order by implementing the 777 Plan.™ With diligence, we will overcome procrastination, break the back of slack, sluggishness and slothfulness, and ultimately we will enter into the land of no lack. If not now then when? This is important because there are so many things God wants to accomplish through us. However, we only have a finite amount of time to accomplish it. Therefore, we should take action now because we do not want our epitaphs to read, *"I woulda', shoulda', coulda'."*

Why Put Off For Tomorrow What God Can Do Today?

Overcome Procrastination, God's Way!

Prayer:

Father I stretch my hands to Thee for there is no other help I know. I stretch my hands and I stretch my heart and mind and I ask You to fill my soul with a surge and a steady stream of Your Dunamis Power! I need to be quickened and strengthened in my inner man so that I may commence and complete my journey of breaking the back of slack and entering into the land of no lack. I need Your Virtue and Your Vitality because I realize that I can do nothing without You. In Jesus' Name, I pray, Amen!

Summary of Scriptures:

Psalm 143:3-4

Ephesians 3:16

Jeremiah 3:25

Romans 8:11

Acts 17:28

Isaiah 40:29

Luke 6:17-19

Luke 8:43-48

Psalm 143:6

Psalm 143:11-12

Exodus 20:11 (NIV)

Exodus 23:12

Proverb 20:13

Proverbs 6:9-11(NKJV)

Ecclesiastes 9:10 (NIV)

†

Epilogue
The Process of Change

Overcoming procrastination is a process of making a real change in our lives. It is a process of complete metamorphosis where our lives take on a totally different appearance and condition. We change from one state of being to another. We change from having lack to no lack and from being inactive to taking action. Ultimately, with change, we break the back of slack, dig out from the past, better manage the present, and eventually we live progressively in the future instead of painfully in the past.

This change must happen deep within. Otherwise, we will revert back to our old slack, slothful and sluggish ways. This type of change cannot happen without help from God. We need His dunamis power to invigorate us as well as help us to overcome whatever looms underneath and causes us to procrastinate.

The best example of change is the metamorphosis of a caterpillar. A caterpillar starts as an egg. Then, it hatches into a caterpillar. Caterpillars, like sloths and slugs, move very slowly and are not very attractive to look at. Then, it takes up residence in a cocoon where it appears nothing is happening. However, while there, transformation takes place. The caterpillar changes into a butterfly and when the metamorphosis is complete, his life is admired and praised by all.

Afterwards, we forget the process he went through to get where he got. So it is with the process we go through when we change from procrastinator to achiever. There are at least three phases of change we go through in order to overcome procrastination. Therefore, it is important to dig a little deeper about what each phase entails. The three phases are:

- **The Caterpillar Phase**
- **The Cocoon Phase**
- **The Butterfly Phase**

The Caterpillar Phase

Many of us live as caterpillars where our lives are under-productive and may not be all that attractive to look at. For most, this phase is very frustrating because things move very slowly and we do not make much progress in our lives. The more we try to get moving; the more we procrastinate. During this phase, we cope with inaction but at the same time we hate it. When we live as caterpillars, we live painfully in the past and we cannot envision

living like butterflies even though, deep down inside, that's what we desire. Nevertheless, the caterpillar phase helps us to make critical decisions that empower us to live the type of lives we want to live.

For example, my first job was at a fast food restaurant. It was harsh work and I made very little money. But, because of that experience, I decided what I did not want to do for the rest of my life. Of course, there was nothing wrong with working there. But after many burns on my hands and arms from the fry machine and clothes smelling of grease every day, I realized that it was not for me. I could not have known that unless I had gone through that experience. So it is with procrastination. I have been a lifelong procrastinator and at some point I decided that I wanted to live peacefully and progressively in the future instead of painfully in the past. I could not have reached that point unless I had lived life as a slack, slothful slug. I hope you have reached that point as well.

We have been through the worst of life but now it is time to experience the best of life. It can be accomplished when we decide to break the back of slack and enter into the land of no lack. We will experience a metamorphosis. Our lives will be transformed to resemble the life of a butterfly and not the life of a caterpillar. However, there is another stage that we may have to endure before we start flying.

The Cocoon Phase

The cocoon phase happens after we have decided to make a change. During this phase, real internal change occurs even if it does not seem like it. Here, we shed our old slack, slothful, and sluggish ways, we establish new habits, and we develop wings with which we are able to fly to new heights in our lives. Here, our diligence is tested as we are forced to muddle and struggle through the growing pains of change. It is not pleasant but it is necessary. Change will not occur unless we go through this transformational part of the process.

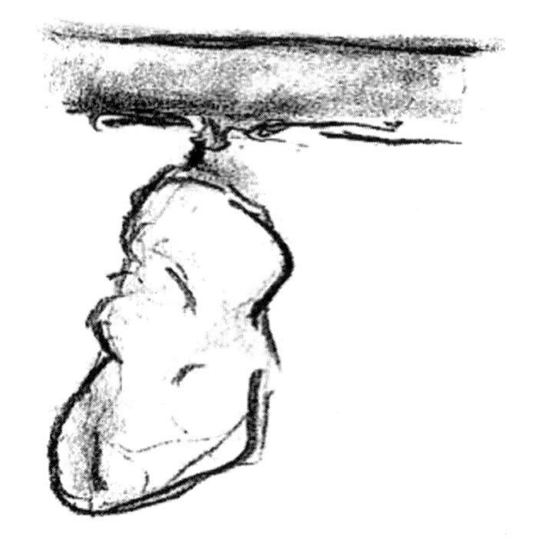

It is much like what a mother goes through when she has been impregnated and then gives birth. The mother must endure a baby growing and kicking in her womb, and she must endure feeling drained of energy because of the changes happening inside of her body. Then, she must endure the excruciating pain that comes from labor. At the same time, she must continue to push until she has given birth. However, all of that pain is forgotten once the beautiful baby has made her transition from living in the womb to living in the world. The same thing happens as we are overcoming procrastination. As part of this process, we will experience some setbacks and roadblocks, and we will experience the winds of resistance which is what happens whenever we want to change the course of our lives. However, the more we muddle and struggle through, the more strength we will gain, and the more we will change for good. That's what happens to the caterpillar when he is in the cocoon. He sheds his old skin and develops strength. His strength is increased each time he hits the side of the cocoon and realizes that he is closer and closer to breaking through and that there is a better way to get where he wants to go—flying instead of crawling.

At some point, his strength will match his desire and as a result he will break through. Nevertheless, even before he breaks through, he realizes that a change took place on the inside and as a result he sees himself as a butterfly. Therefore, no longer can he fathom living life as a slack, slothful, sluggish caterpillar. He begins to believe that he can get out of the cocoon and take his flight to the land of no lack. So it is with us, after we have muddled and struggled a while, our strength will match our desire and our diligence will transform our desires into accomplishments. We will break through. We will overcome negative thinking; fear, worry and shame, and lack of order. We will begin to see ourselves as butterflies and not caterpillars even if the process is violent, or at least painful. However, it will not matter because our pain will soon be forgotten once we begin to fly.

The Butterfly Phase

When we start flying, we will need to continue flying and living as butterflies. That means we will need to maintain our new lifestyle by continuing to implement The 777 Plan.™ We will need to realize that we are no longer caterpillars (sloths or slugs) instead we are butterflies (diligent, high-flying achievers). That means we must continue to flap our new wings and fly higher and higher while resting along the way to appreciate the beauty of the things that have changed around us. Also, we must continue to live progressively in the future instead of allowing the present to become the past or the past to become the present. In other words, we must continue to live a no lack existence. However, we must realize it is a journey and not a destination. But, the journey is a much better journey than the one we took when we were procrastinators. Therefore, commence your journey, overcome procrastination God's way, break the back of slack, enter the land of no lack, and do not look back.

You can obtain all forms found in this book, and other helpful materials by logging onto: http://www.The777Plan.com

For updates on new products and services of i611 Press, LLC, log onto: http://www.i611Press.com